THIS GOSPEL OF THE KINGDOM

THIS GOSPEL OF THE KINGDOM

GEORGE S. GUNN
Photo by Lafayette

THIS GOSPEL OF THE KINGDOM

Dilemmas in Evangelism

by

GEORGE S. GUNN

Edited by
PROFESSOR NORMAN W. PORTEOUS, D.D.
New College, Edinburgh

Foreword by
THE VERY REV. PROFESSOR JAMES S. STEWART, D.D.
Moderator of the Church of Scotland, 1963–64

JAMES CLARKE & CO. LTD
33 Store Street
London, W.C.1

First published 1964

Printed in Great Britain at the St Ann's Press
Park Road, Altrincham

To

ST. ANDREW'S CHURCH
JUNIPER GREEN

and

BROUGHTON PLACE CHURCH
EDINBURGH

my two
dear and faithful
Congregations

Acknowledgments

I am very happy to record my great debt and deep thanks to Miss Mabel Isdale, who, with all speed and accuracy, typed a manuscript which provided no evidence of the fact that the author once in early life received a handsome prize for excellence in handwriting.

Special acknowledgment is made to the following: Dr. William Steven for taking down the Preface and the latter part of the book in shorthand as Dr. Gunn dictated it to him; to the Very Rev. Professor James S. Stewart, D.D., for writing the Foreword, and to Professor Norman W. Porteous, D.D., for reading the typescript and correcting the proofs.

Contents

Foreword

HERE is a book on evangelism from the pen of one whose whole ministry was evangelism. It was a wonderful gift God gave the Scottish Church in George Sinclair Gunn. Through every stage of his life-work—from the family worship of his early Caithness home and the brilliant years at University and College, to the multifarious tasks of a great city parish and the wider service of the Church at home and abroad, and right on to the triumphant close—there kept sounding the authentic apostolic "This one thing I do." Never surely was there a man more fully possessed with a sense of the sheer exhilaration of the Christian ministry: every common day was brimful of interest, "a day of God's own contriving," and therefore to be offered back to God in resolute consecration and with an undivided will. It was an extraordinarily impressive achievement that one so immersed in the practical affairs of the Church—including the Convenership of such important Assembly Committees as Foreign Missions and Education for the Ministry—should have contrived to maintain throughout his ministry the scholarly habits acquired at University and College: his library was indeed his only extravagance. The Cunningham Lectures he delivered in 1944 bore fruit in his notable volume on "The Doctrine of God in the Psalms." Of the present book on evangelism it ought to be known— this surely is a very moving fact which will give these pages an added significance—that the final paragraphs were written on his deathbed with immense difficulty but indomitable courage less than a week before the end.

There must be scores of men in the Church to-day to

whom through George Gunn there was given, under God, the call to the holy ministry. As a preacher, he magnified his office; and in a day when sermons keep on dwindling in bulk and perhaps shrinking in theological content to suit the taste of a somewhat restive generation, he would make no apology for preaching for forty-five minutes, and what is more, he would hold his Congregation's attention from the first words to the last. His pastoral work was of the first order: no statistics can record the fruit of those long hours he spent in personal evangelism, often far into the night. His was indeed a notable example of a truly Christian stewardship of time, talents and possessions: he could never say No to anyone in need, and again and again he gave to the point of sacrifice and self-impoverishment. He could be forthright and out-spoken in defence of principle; yet he carried about him a wonderful gentleness and a strange and even shy reserve. His last months on earth, when we knew he was leaving us, were characterised by the courage and serenity and triumph one would expect in such a man of God. We will always remember our brother George with love and gratitude; and through these pages on the dilemmas of evangelism we can hear the personal witness of one who was the true pattern of an evangelist.

JAMES S. STEWART

Preface

In the first year or two of my undertaking the tasks of the ministry I found two deep concerns in my mind.

The first, with which this book does not deal, is the place of pastoral work. The real battle of the Church goes on in the congregation. The discussions and decisions of the Church in its higher courts, convocations and assemblies, are always secondary and auxiliary. If they are to take on life it must be in the congregation and so there is a central priority for the pastor's work. But we live in an age of social patterns which make this very difficult. The Church has to look for means to restore pastoral work to its central importance.

The second concern is the age-long problem of relating what we hold in our personal faith to the complicated world situation around us; and the world situation is growing more complicated. Quite early in my ministry I found that many people in the Church simply feel that this cannot be done. So they consciously or unconsciously divide up their life into compartments—what they try to hold as a personal faith on Sunday, and what they feel they have to live as men of the world. Life for many can be described as mainly secular, with a small decorative fringe of varying pattern stitched on round the edge. Here is a jagged problem which has torn the conscience of people all through the Christian ages. This book is intended to deal with it. It is a theological issue, but an attempt is here made to present the theological issue so that constructive expository preaching may be given to it. That is the joy of life.

GEORGE S. GUNN

11

CHAPTER ONE

The Full Gospel

IT IS the very fullness of the Christian Gospel that makes it "glad tidings to every creature". Accordingly the Christian Church which is God's appointed instrument for communicating the Gospel to every creature is required continually to remind itself that the choice before men is always the full Gospel or no Gospel at all.

There is no section of man's life in which it can be seriously maintained that one man's view is as good as another's. Least of all is that conceivable in religion. It is essential to the Christian religion that it is not in any sense the product of human thinking, for its vital truths are such that man by his unaided efforts would never have conceived them. Christianity, in New Testament terms, is a "mystery" —not just something hard to understand, but impossible to understand unless it has been given and revealed by God, a secret which is now open to men because God has chosen to disclose it.

It is utterly different, therefore, from being a matter of opinion. There is a place in life for opinions, but there is a more important and decisive place for convictions. The difference between an opinion and a conviction is that we do and must change our opinions, perhaps frequently and easily, but our deepest convictions can and must change and make us. The Gospel is not to be classed among matters of taste and fancy but stands in the central place around which cluster truth and fact, obedience and duty, faith and vision. Mr. Andrew Carnegie, addressing the students of St. Andrews University, declared that, as he grew older, he had "less theology, but more reverence". What he surely meant was that he attached less value to the changing forms of theology, not to theology itself as the quest and expression of truth. It would be wholly false and contradictory to say "less truth and more reverence". The Christian Gospel has not hesitated to present itself as absolute and final truth, which consequently confronts all men with a decision and calls for the response of the whole being. It is a full Gospel because its only source is in God, "the glorious Gospel of the blessed God" (1 Tim. 1, 11), because it is incarnate in an eternal, supernatural Person, Jesus Christ, because it gathers up in perfect fulfilment all the best that went before it, because it leads the individual believer into the abundant life, and because it brings a dynamic touch and an unfolding hope to every area of human activity.

There are modern critics of the Christian religion, some of them with a good education, who would not hesitate to say that we could no more revive Christianity in the present world than we could revive witchcraft. They have a quite irrational fear of the transcendent, the supernatural and the miraculous, combined with an excessively rationalist attitude to life which seeks to exclude all mystery and to claim that goodness is in fact attainable without any Divine support or sanction. On these rocks people have been going shipwreck in all ages, and in still larger numbers in our time. Beyond this, modern criticism of the Christian religion is directed not so much against the full substance of it as against some distortion of it produced by taking some part of it for the whole, some absurd excrescence identified with an extreme and unrepresentative individual, or some theological formulation now long out of date. Such a situation is not eased but made worse by all tendencies to water down the Gospel, to make the narrow way much wider and to cut drastically both the gracious promise and the inexorable demand of the Gospel. All this has to be countered by a confident and vigorous proclamation of the Gospel as a grand and majestic whole, and not, as an incisive novel *The Evangelists* puts it, "by stepping from thought to thought on pious stilts".

2

For many years now there has been proceeding a re-awakening of Biblical study of a much deeper quality than in the preceding period. A great deal of very close attention has been given to drawing out from the New Testament documents the essential Gospel and to the demonstration of the basic unity of the Bible in terms of the essential Gospel. In this connection one of the most valuable pioneer books is "The Apostolic Preaching and its Developments" by C. H. Dodd. Published in 1936, its argument has been expanded by Dr. Dodd in later books and by many other writers whom he has inspired.

At the root of Dr. Dodd's discussion lies the clear distinction drawn by the New Testament writers between "preaching" (kerygma) and "teaching" (didache). The former is the very substance of the good news which has to be proclaimed to men; the latter is moral instruction and exhortation which had to be given to the converts whom it pleased God to save by the "preaching", not by the "teaching" (1 Cor. 1, 21). From the preaching of the early Church, as revealed in Acts and the Epistles, the outline of the essential Gospel is stated by Dr. Dodd as follows:

> The prophecies are fulfilled, and the new Age is
> inaugurated by the coming of Christ.
> He was born of the seed of David.
> He died according to the Scriptures, to deliver
> us out of the present evil age.

15

He was buried.
He rose on the third day according to the Scriptures.
He is exalted at the right hand of God, as Son of God
and Lord of quick and dead.
He will come again as Judge and Saviour of men.

The passages in which this essential Gospel is most completely expressed are Acts 2, 14–39; 3, 13–26; 4, 10–12; 5, 30–32; 10, 36–43; 13, 17–41. Gal. 1, 3–4; 3, 1; 4, 6; 1 Thess. 1, 10; 1 Cor. 15, 1–7; Romans 1, 1–4; 8, 34; 2, 16; 10, 8–9. The whole New Testament clings around this tremendous core; and for its supreme sake the Christian Church was founded, all the New Testament documents written and treasured, and the Old Testament accepted as Christian Scriptures in due course. The preaching of Peter and Paul, as recorded in Acts, reveals that there is fundamental agreement among all the apostles as to the immense affirmations of the Gospel, and that the source of it all is the Person and the message of our Lord. The more study that is given to what we find proclaimed by our Lord in the Gospels and by the apostles in the rest of the New Testament, the more overwhelming is the evidence for the astonishing unity of the witness.

It is of special value to dwell a little longer on some of Paul's ways of dealing with the Gospel. He does not hesitate to describe it as "my Gospel"—"God shall judge the secrets of men by Jesus Christ according to my Gospel" (Romans 2, 16); "remember that Jesus Christ of the seed of David was raised from the dead according to my Gospel" (2 Tim. 2, 8). Judgment is by Jesus Christ who alone can bring to light what men really are, and the basis of judgment is the Gospel for those who have heard it. Paul regards the Gospel as something to be made known everywhere, the highest blessing available to men, and so he had a deep fear of "making the Gospel of none effect", and he was always aware of the danger of lapsing into "another Gospel" (Gal. 1, 1–6). He has "received" the Gospel, and because of its very character there is none other way than that if we are to have it at all.

Yet it is no presumption to describe it as "my Gospel". For the Gospel made Paul what he was, radically changed his life and gave him blazing enthusiasm for a cause that once he despised and persecuted. After his conversion he had to spend his whole life facing a hard, hostile world, with hindrances on every side, and threats of extinction waiting round every corner for him and the young Church. But his experience was that nothing can effectively stop the Gospel, and the whole story of Acts and the autobiographical references in the Epistles emphasise that splendid conviction. From the Gospel he draws the power to face the world—"I can do all things through Christ who strengtheneth me" (Phil. 4, 13). Paul's missionary achievement, under Christ, was immense; none can blame him if he speaks almost boastfully of his mission work in many far-spread fields, to which indeed there is no parallel in Christian history. His own response of personal faith and dedication was so profound that he is entitled on that score too to say "my Gospel". It was his to keep and his to give, his to cherish and his to share. Because he did both so well, the world has yet to show a better Christian than Paul.

In the first chapter of Romans, Paul indicates that the opportunity of preaching the Gospel in Rome would be the very crown and consummation of his missionary career, "for I am not ashamed of the Gospel of Christ, it is the power of God unto salvation to everyone that believeth, to the Jew first and also to the Greek" (Romans 1, 15–16). This urgent desire to confront Rome with the Gospel is the striking measure of his pride in the Gospel. He himself had once been ashamed of it (1 Cor. 1, 19–31), but after his conversion he would never let slip out of his mind the words of Jesus Christ with their piercing, sombre reminder that He too may be ashamed of us (Mark 8, 38; Luke 9, 26). Paul knew only too well that Imperial Rome would have nothing but contempt and antagonism to the kind of Gospel he had to preach, but he also had no doubt that every worldly power or empire that sets itself to destroy the Gospel and the Church is attempting the impossible and sealing its own downfall. He was confident that there are forces in the Gospel, truth, love, goodness, which are more powerful and enduring than the forces of worldly strength, arbitrary power and violence upon which an earthly kingdom or empire comes to rely too much; and so the Gospel abides and spreads long after the earthly realms and regimes crash. The persistent survival of Christianity is the most impressive fact of two thousand years.

When Paul glories in the Gospel, he is thinking not of what God has yet to do, but of what He has already done. Moreover, the Gospel is not merely what man wants, for there is no particular reason for being proud of that, but what man most urgently needs. As such there is and can only be one Gospel. When we speak of the old-fashioned Gospel and the new-fashioned Gospel, we are at best referring only to different ways of stating the Gospel. Or, when we speak of the personal and the social Gospel, we mean only that there are both personal and social implications and obligations of the Gospel. The one Gospel is that, to men who are in a plight through sin in which they are powerless to help themselves, God has come to their rescue. There has been an invasion from heaven to earth, a Divine intervention of our natural order from the supernatural order. This has been done in Jesus Christ and in His fulfilment of God's preparation for His coming. In Christ God has taken upon Himself the whole, dreadful burden of human sin, suffering and sorrow—good news indeed, to which there is no counterpart anywhere at all.

Paul grasps this Gospel in terms of power—the power of God unto salvation. The power resides in what the Gospel of Christ alone declares to men and makes possible for them. Paul had faithfully sought a way of deliverance by the works of the Jewish law, but he had failed and still remained a "wretched man" (Romans 7, 24–25). The Gospel makes a fourfold declaration to man. First, that man's inherent restlessness can be satisfied only by getting into personal touch with One higher than himself. All human beings belong in a real sense to the family of God, "the offspring of God" (Acts 17, 28). But that relationship takes on a new quality after conversion. Some sons are yet in darkness, some have welcomed the light; some are in obedience, some in rebellion; some are at home with the Father, some are in a far country. But all are sons, and nothing can alter that. We are saved or lost as sons. Secondly, in the Gospel is a declaration of true independence. Man is continually exposed to the temptation of seeking a false independence, striving to convince himself that he stands in need of nothing except what he himself can provide. As man lives in that way, he loses self-control, becomes helpless in face of many fierce temptations and allows life to become master of him. In the Gospel there is power for man to become master of life, to regain self-control and to conquer temptation. Thirdly, in the Gospel is a declaration of unity—"it is to the Jew first but also to the Greek". In Paul's world the gulf between Jew and Gentile was the deepest and widest of all. But in Christ it is bridged and transcended, and likewise all the barriers and boundaries of human society can be surmounted in Him. Even as the three continents of the known world were represented together on the day of the Cross—the penitent thief from Asia, the Roman Centurion from Europe, and Simon of Cyrene from Africa, and even as the Cross made them one, so the whole world, sorely divided, can be unified in Him. The urgent choice before mankind is a Christian world-order or no sure and lasting world-order at all. Fourthly, in the Gospel is a declaration of a great destiny for believing men. In the world of Nature around us, all that man can see is that there is some power that brings us into life, into a world that is well adapted for life, some power that cares for and provides for us, gives us many chances to develop and then seems to weary of us and sets about supplying some means for our enfeeblement and destruction. We travel for a time along a road which can be fascinatingly interesting—and then the inevitable grave. Nature itself has no answer to this or any other deep question, but the Gospel has an answer to them all. In all four respects, the Gospel is "the Great Charter" of the soul.

One final example of Paul's attitude to the Gospel is to be found in Acts 17, 16–34. His mission to Athens was not a total failure, but it was not a notable success. There is no trace in the New Testament of "the Church which is at Athens" nor is there an "Epistle to the Athenians". For Paul, the Gospel was nothing less than a lifeline, but for most of the people who heard Paul preach at Athens it was at most a sideline, one among many. He never encountered more difficult hearers than these. They were ready for an argument about anything, and if it was something new, so much the better. But there was no real desire for the discovery of truth, no readiness to put the truth into action, no willingness to be different people. To them Paul was just "another professional peddler of ideas", and speculative ideas were the diet that they favoured. The Gospel, as Paul preached it, did not encourage people to close their minds or dethrone their reason; and yet it was such that argument alone could convert nobody. Except for the silent scorn of the intellectual snob and the cool indifference of the easy-going procrastinator, Paul's preaching provoked no opposition or persecution in Athens.

The apostle, ever willing to be all things to all men that he might win some, goes out of his way to impress upon people like the Athenians that the very idea of God is a lifeline, not a sideline. "In Him we live and move and have our being"—which means that our bodily existence, our faculties and the exercise of them, and our individual life as a self-conscious being ever seeking self-realizaton come to us from God Himself. There are sidelines in life which are pleasant, interesting, enriching and profitable—but they are not the main business of life. True religion is a necessity, not a luxury, and without it people are just nibbling around the edges of reality. According to the Christian Gospel, we touch full, final reality not in money, pleasure or popularity—but when we encounter the God of our salvation in His Son. God is Creator, Redeemer and Judge (Acts 17, 31) and that is supreme reality. The Gospel, as Paul understood it, is a life-line in a twofold sense—as a means of supply of what is essential to the good life, and as a means of rescue from what is dangerous to voyagers on the sea of this world.

3

The evidence of the entire Bible is that the situation which God had and has to deal with is a lost and fallen world. The human situation to which the Gospel is addressed is an utterly sinful one, affecting deeply every area of man's life. Sin is "a knot which only a God can unravel", and it requires the almightiness and the sublimity of Perfect Holy Love to save sinners. God has undertaken that task, and He is continually at work in ways of creative love to fulfil it.

It is much too mild a statement of the case to say that man is far from what he ought to be. The doctrine of the Fall which stands at the opening of the Bible and to which the whole Bible is related must be taken much more seriously than that. According to the Scriptures, the human race has taken a dreadfully wrong turn, the very character of which is a selfish, self-willed, conscious resistance to the Divine Will. Some people find Genesis 3 one of the most perplexing chapters in the Bible. While the form has to be distinguished from the substance of this story, there is no doubt what the substance is, nor of its exact, urgent relevance to all men. Man, given his life by God in a world prepared for his coming, claims his independence, becomes a rebel against God, defies what his Creator intended him to be, chooses the very opposite of what his Maker said was good, and embarks on a way of life the end of which is death. As

21

Werner Pelz puts it in a singularly incisive book "Irreligious Reflections on the Christian Church", "Man commits the incredible folly of believing the first beast to cross his path rather than the God who made him. He makes a gesture of utter futility in response to God's gesture of unreserved graciousness. But God contradicts our contradictions, His love rebels against our rebellion". God considers the possibility of bringing to an end completely what he had begun, "I will destroy man whom I have created" (Gen. 6, 5–7). Instead, He undertakes the task of making men anew, and the whole Bible contains the account of God's action to redeem and save. If the story of the Fall was not at the beginning of the Bible, it would be impossible to understand what the whole Bible is about. In contrast to all man-centred confidence and to all the distorted superficialities of Marxism, the Bible maintains that man is "the glory and the scum of the world" (Pascal). We are all involved in Adam's fall. In that dark sense, Adam is Everyman. Man, the crown of the Creator's work, made in His image, endowed with gifts which no other creature possesses, capable of the inward response of fellowship and obedience, thinks that he knows better than God, and seeks in pride and self-glorying to usurp God's place (Romans 1, 22–23). So there is now in God's world a realm of evil over against the realm of good.

In the chapters of Genesis which describe conditions after the fall, we have a picture of a society in which every relationship is disturbed, consequent upon the fatal break of communication with God. Every breakdown has to be connected with this original breakdown. With clear insight and in vivid terms this is all portrayed—self-assertion against each other, throwing the blame on the other person, the vain attempt to hide from God, the acceptance of work as a curse and nuisance rather than a blessing and privilege, strife, drunkenness, lust and murder—such is the harvest of the conflict of man's will with God. The serpent represents the hideous subtlety of temptation. It suggests to Adam and Eve that there is good cause to doubt the Creator's goodness, it makes God appear to be jealous in keeping His knowledge to Himself, and it appeals to human vanity with the vision of their being like gods and setting themselves up at the centre of the universe.

But God cannot let fallen man go and suffer the full consequences of the Fall. Instead He calls to Adam, and Adam is not beyond the reach of the Creator's voice (cf. Psalm 139). In that sense it was not a fall into total depravity, for he is still capable of hearing and responding. That is true of all who have shared in Adam's fall—at least for a time. The sentence of death, consequent upon sin, has been justly passed, but God now sets Himself to find a way to reverse and cancel that sentence.

The divine purpose of redemption works itself out stage by stage in the election of Israel, and now in the new Israel which is the Church of Christ, and so it will proceed until the final consummation of all things. In the fullness of the times, at the time and place that God knew to be best, the second Adam appears (Romans 5, 15–21; 1 Cor. 15, 22, 45–49). God goes out to seek His lost children—"as in Adam, so in Christ". Sin abounded, but redeeming grace much more abounded. The judgment in Eden was terrible and far-reaching, but the free gift in Christ is immeasurably superior and more far-reaching. By one man sin and death entered the world, and by one man righteousness and life entered. Adam attempted disastrously for himself and all his race to grasp at God's glory, but Christ regarded His glory with the Father not as a thing to be clutched and held on to, but to be laid aside so that He, having thus emptied Himself, might be made in the likeness of men (Phil. 2, 5–11). Adam stands at the head of the fallen race, Christ at the head of the redeemed race.

We have a Gospel because God has spoken and acted in Holy Love for the redemption and salvation of men. He has not waited until sinful man himself chose to do something about it. He has come out upon the long search; by grace He is first in the field "Last of all I will send my Son" (Mark

12, 1–11); "the Son of Man is come to seek and to save that which was lost" (Luke 19, 10). Some interpreters of the parable of the younger son (Luke 15, 11–24), after bringing out the rich meanings for us, have gone on to say that it is defective in that it does not express the complete Gospel, and that by it alone we shall not secure a full grasp of essential Christianity. The parable, however, spoken by One who was on His way to Calvary to vindicate by a deed of perfect self-sacrifice the love of the Father which He has expressed in that story, is a true picture both of man's plight as a sinner and of God's attitude to the sinner. God deals with sinners not in strict, legal justice, the way of the elder brother, but in infinite grace; otherwise no one could have any standing or hope before Him. The leading character in the parable is not the son but the father, going forth to meet him when he was still a great way off and providing for him a welcome and a renewal out of all relationship to his deserts. So we are taught that no conception is more out of place in true religion than merit. We are not saved because we deserve it, nor because we have earned it and have a right to it. "There is no task more cheerless than that of trying to earn the love without which we cannot live". Although Jesus does not literally say that the father travelled to the far country to seek and save the lost son, that is indeed its true meaning. The God who runs to receive penitent sinners is, in Paul's language, the God who "justifies the ungodly"; and it is all of grace.

On the eve of the Cross, Jesus Christ made a statement which is the most startling word of the New Testament— "that the world may know that thou hast loved them as thou hast loved me" (John 17, 23). The Father loves us all even as He loves His Son; and, as He loved Him "from the foundation of the world" (John 17, 24), so in Christ He loves us from the foundation of the world. This is the one place where Christ and we stand equal. In every other way we are essentially inferior—in our knowledge of the things of God, in our personal moral character, in our service to humanity—for in

24

all these fields He is not only easily first but altogether unique. The source of man's true dignity and of the sanctity of personality lies here—that God has set upon us the same love as He has set upon His only-begotten Son.

This casts a flood of light upon the love of God. It shows how unlike human love God's love is. Jesus was to the Father what none of us can ever be—"His own" in a special sense. We are not capable of loving everybody as we love our own, even when we are best disposed to all our fellow-creatures. And yet this word reveals how wonderfully like God's Love is to human love at its highest, e.g. in a good mother. Perhaps the only place in the world where it can be said that all within the circle are the same to the presiding love is a family of several children, all unlike each other, but all equal in the mother's love which indeed is often capable of showing a sort of special tenderness to the wayward. In one passage and one only is God's Love explicitly likened to a mother's, "as one whom his mother comforteth, so will I comfort thee" (Isaiah 66, 13). God, as revealed in Christ, is able to take up that attitude to all who live. That is indeed first on the list of the "all things which are possible with God" (Mark 10, 27). The Bible on several occasions, however, tells us that there are "impossibles" in God's vocabulary too —and one of them has to be stressed here. While Perfect Love cannot give itself in part or by measure to anyone, but has to offer itself completely to everyone, no more can it drive or force the sinner to faith, obedience and goodness. While no one can be saved outside the grace of God, and while it is a task for the whole omnipotence of God to save a soul, God is unable ultimately to treat the penitent believer and the rebellious unbeliever as if there was no difference between them, for that would be to deny Himself and to violate His own very nature. But it is certain that, when a man accepts such a love as this, it soon shows itself productive of great good in his life. It helps him to accept the suffering of life, even if it is a mystery, for he looks to the suffering of the Cross. He is lifted above the divisions of life, the tensions and resentments against those who have hurt us, the deep difference of conviction often accompanied by dislike or malice, the gulf created by class, occupation or race. We dare not ignore, despise or hate anyone whom God loves as He loves His Son. Life is taken with proper seriousness as a great business, moved by the inspiration of a grand hope, and lived out in high and happy earnestness, when the light of such a love shines upon it.

But it is also plain that God understands how hard it is for man to believe in such a Love as this. It is not easy and natural for the natural man to love and serve God. Most people know well that it seemed easier and more natural in childhood, and that is why we have to be converted and become childlike, not childish, again. Nor is it easy and natural for the natural man to believe that God loves us with a personal, sacrificial love. There are so many stubborn facts that appear to deny such a faith, and there is no assurance to be found just by surveying life in general. The temptation of the natural man is always to by-pass the Cross, to keep sacrifice and suffering far off for as long as possible. These two attitudes can be broken down only at the Cross.

The term "love" is never actually used by Jesus in the synoptic gospels to describe God's relationship to us, and yet that thought is structural to the Gospel. The early Christians exulted in it, published it, trumpeted it, because of Christ's vicarious death, a sacrifice well-pleasing and fragrant to God (Ephes. 5, 2). The Cross was in the heart of God from all eternity—"The Lamb slain from the foundation of the world" (Rev. 13, 8). "God commendeth His love toward us in that while we were yet sinners, Christ died for us" (Romans 5, 8). That is a text, which like John 3, 16, has everything in it. God's chief desire is to get sinners to accept His love, but He knows that it has to be commended to us, urged upon us, and there is no length to which He will not go to achieve that. "In due time, when we were without strength, Christ died for the ungodly" (Romans 5, 6). When man was weak and helpless, Christ died for them, "at the right time" (R.S.V.), "at the decisive moment" (Goodspeed). God proves and verifies His love, in a world where it needs much proving and verifying, by the death of His Son. The Cross flings its challenge out against all the dark facts that of themselves challenge God's love, and it is the final proof of that love. God has other ways of showing His love—in the beauty and bounty of creation, the dependable gifts and mercies of daily Providence, His unseen control and guidance of life, His patience with evil people, and in all the lovely and saintly lives. But not all these together are sufficient. He allows His Son to go and die, and the Father goes through Golgotha with the Son. "By this we know what love is, because He laid down His life for us" (1 John 3, 16). It is not a helpless Victim who is dragged to the Cross—"no man taketh my life from me, I lay it down of myself. I have power to lay it down and I have power to take it again; this commandment have I received from my father" (John 10, 18). Nor is it to change God's attitude to sinners or to appease an angry God, as if God's attitude was less merciful or more just than the Son's, for the Father never loved the Son more than when He laid down His life (John 10, 17). In His sacrifice of perfect obedience, He took upon Himself the pains and sufferings which rightly fall upon sinners, though He was no sinner. Paul agonized to express this in the great passage dealing with our reconciliation to God and the cost of it to Christ (2 Cor. 5, 18–21).

It is Paul also who brings us to the astonishing assurance that our relationship to Christ in the Gospel is utterly personal. "Christ loved us and gave Himself for us" (Ephes. 5, 2). "God who is rich in mercy, for His great love wherewith He loved us" (Ephes. 2, 4). That is personal in the plural, but He goes on to make it personal in the singular in Gal. 2, 20— "I am crucified with Christ; nevertheless I live; yet not I, but Christ liveth in me: and the life which I now live in the flesh, I live by the faith of the Son of God, who loved me and gave himself for me". The strongest possible emphasis must be placed on "me"—and then we are in a position to ask "Lord, what wilt thou have me to do?" (Acts 9, 6). The Gospel is perceived in its fullness when a man reads his own name into "me", and he makes the great discovery that it was for him that Christ came from heaven to earth, endured persecution and privation, passed through Gethsemane, was beaten with rods, spit upon, mocked and taunted, deserted and forsaken, had nails driven into his flesh, and died and was buried—and raised again and exalted and given the name Lord which is above every name. This is a Love to fill us with gratitude, humility, fear, hope, wonder. Here is the deep source of what Dr. Kagawa called "the master-miracle of me". Apart from this miraculous outpouring of God's Love, there is no Gospel. By it our condemnation is taken away, we are adopted as sons (Romans 8, 1–17). "He has delivered us from the dominion of darkness and translated us into the kingdom of His dear Son" (Col. 1, 13).

4

The charge of intolerance has often been made against Christianity. In the true sense of the word, this charge is the glory of the Gospel. "Neither is there salvation in any other, for there is none other name under heaven given among men whereby we must be saved" (Acts 4, 12). In that there is a unique, sublime intolerance; but it is a sad fact that frequently in history evil and ugly methods of intolerance have been employed to advance this splendid claim. Christianity is presented to man as the final and absolute religion. It is not necessary to dismiss the other great religions of mankind as totally false, but it is necessary to maintain that in their basic conceptions they are not nearly good enough. It will not do, after the manner of Toynbee and others, to hold up the hope of some ultimate syncretistic amalgamation of all the higher religions. There is a timeless character about the Gospel. It is no more possible to bring the Gospel up-to-date than it is to bring God up-to-date.

To the careful reader of the New Testament it is piercingly obvious that there is a "once-for-all" character in the Gospel. Such a thing as this can never confidently be said of any form of human speech or action, but it can and must be said of God's speech and action in Christ. "He died unto sin once for all" (Romans 6, 10). "This he did once for all when he offered up himself" (Heb. 7, 27). "Christ was offered once for all to bear the sins of many" (Heb. 9, 28). "By his own blood he entered in once for all into the holy place, having obtained eternal redemption for us" (Heb. 9, 12). "Now once for all in the end of the world hath he appeared to put away sin by the sacrifice of himself" (Heb. 9, 26). "We are sanctified through the offering of the body of Jesus Christ once for all" (Heb. 10, 10). "He died once for all, the just for the unjust, that he might bring us to God" (1 Peter 3, 18). The Son of God need not and will not die on a Cross again. The old, imperfect sacrifices of Israel are superseded, for they were essentially ineffectual. The perfect sacrifice has been made, and it is unrepeatable. "I have finished the work which thou gavest me to do" (John 17, 4). The dreadful impasse created by sin has been broken and a completely new start is possible, and fallen man can have oneness with God again. The redemption wrought by Christ is universal, not limited; but salvation as a felt and experienced fact tarries till men repent and accept their redemption in Him.

What is so emphatically stressed in these passages in respect of the death of Christ is equally true of all the events in His life from His birth at Bethlehem to His ascension at Olivet—all the events that had to take place before the Holy Spirit could be sent down to illumine, guide, and energise the Church. These events form one coherent drama of Divine Love in action, and there is in them the same divine necessity as there was in His death (Matt. 16, 21). Perfect Love must find a way of making itself incarnate before men. Inasmuch as the Incarnation takes place in an evil world, tension, conflict and suffering are inevitable, to the point of the Cross. But Perfect Love must triumph over that; and the faith, obedience and sacrifice of the Son must be vindicated and rewarded here in this world and in the eternal world—and so the Cross must issue in the Resurrection and Ascension. The hope and promise given to Israel are now re-asserted in a complete form, and in Acts and in Paul's letters that light shines steadily and powerfully. The significance of the Resurrection and the Ascension is supreme here—"we are born again into a living hope by the resurrection of Jesus Christ from the dead" (1 Peter 1, 3). The Risen Lord is seated at the Father's right hand in the place of dignity and authority. Only once in the New Testament is He represented as standing at the Father's right hand, at the death of Stephen (Acts 7, 56), as if He had stood up to welcome and honour the first martyr of the Gospel. There too He carries on continuously His ministry of intercession for us (Heb. 7, 24–25; Romans 8, 33–4; 1 John 2, 1; Rev. 5, 13). Dr. James Denney in "Studies in Theology" (p. 162) describes this aspect of the Ascension as something which the apostles refer to "with a kind of adoring awe which is quite peculiar even in the New Testament, one of the unimaginable wonders of redemption". The Ascension stands for the award to Jesus of the supreme place in the whole universe, when He had accomplished the perfect completion of His redeeming work. Following on it, an entirely new relationship with Him is available for believers, dependent no longer on His visible presence. Beyond description in words, but known by its powerful effects, the Ascension is a perpetual inspiration to the Church. It is the festival which, in "the Biblical rhythm" holds all the other festivals together.

No one except a wholehearted believer in the Gospel would ever understand that the world's decisive hour is now past. If it were in the future, there might be little that we could say of it. But it does not lie beyond us, nor is it to be looked for even in the revolutionary, apocalyptic present in which we live. In Mark 1, 14–15, we are given what is virtually the text on which Jesus Christ preached His first sermon. Having made a complete dedication to His mission and an open association of Himself with sinners in the Baptism of Jordan (though He had no personal need of the baptism of repentance) and having rejected in the temptations of the wilderness all the false methods of achieving His purposes for men, He returns in the power of the Spirit and opens His public campaign. The passage can be translated "The hour has struck, the Kingdom of God is here, repent and believe the Gospel". That is the unalterable, unsurpassable "Gospel of the Kingdom of God". That is evangelism in its complete substance, from its beginning to its end.

The appearing of Jesus Christ and His mission to the world constitute the greatest turning-point in history. Something has happened which will vitally affect and determine all history till history reaches its close. What God has to say to men and to do for men has been actually present in our world in its complete and final form in the events of the birth, life, death, resurrection and ascension of Christ. All subsequent events in time have to be related to these decisive events either positively or negatively, by acceptance or rejection. Whether they know it or not, humanity has crossed its watershed—and that remains true irrespective of how long and far human history may yet be extended.

All that went before was the preparation for the decisive hour, and especially in the development of Israel, from the call of Abraham onwards, stage by stage. It is the day which many kings and prophets desired to see but did not see (Luke 10, 23). This zero-hour, this final crisis of intervention, was chosen by God (Gal. 4, 4; Ephes. 1, 10). When Jesus sent out His disciples, it was to publish this Gospel of the Kingdom (Matt. 10, 7–8; Luke 10, 9–11). The new age of the Kingdom is present in all His acts of compassion and power, in His conflict with the rigid upholders of tradition, in His distinctive teaching about the good life and in the resources of spiritual power available in Himself to men of faith and obedience. It is the final opportunity for mankind, inasmuch as to the end of time a better opportunity is inconceivable. God's utter best has been done. So He challenges all men to repentance and belief. What He asks here—full, deep change of thoughts and desires. and a faith in Him which is given with the loyal consent of all our faculties—is comparatively rare in our world. It is never possible to separate repenting and believing. In making such an emphasis, Jesus linked Himself with the mission of John the Baptist; and when Peter and Paul preach the Gospel, it is with precisely these accents. Repentance and faith will bring anyone anywhere at any time into a Kingdom that will not pass away. By repentance and faith we belong to the new age and at length will share its blessedness and triumph; without them we are still in the old age and will share its misery and judgment. Jesus Christ is offered to all men as Saviour if they will only accept Him; but all men must have Him as Judge. So the greatest of all texts is John 3, 16.

5

It is of great importance to grasp the precise form in which the Gospel confronts men. Professor Farmer in "God and the World" develops in a powerful argument the thesis that God is apprehended by us as "absolute demand and final succour". Might it not be more Scriptural to say "Gracious offer, absolute demand and final succour". One sure test of whether we are becoming better Christians and growing nearer to God is the extent to which the conception of God's gifts commands the mind and stirs the soul. It is too easy to fumble with or actually resist the thought that it is all the gift of God. "Every good and perfect gift is from above and comes down from the Father of lights" (James 1, 17). The

Christian religion is put wholly out of focus when its demands are presented first, and for this reason many people suspect and misunderstand it. The demand is just impossible without the prior offer. But the Bible holds the two ideas in inseparable unity. Forgiveness and eternal life are offered by God to men, to be received by faith and surrender, and that in turn blossoms in obedience, sacrifice and worship. This is the golden clasp which holds together not only the New Testament but the whole Bible.

All Creation, with its beauties and bounties, its resources and riches, is the gift of God to men who are left free to enjoy them, to use them or abuse them; and this extends far beyond the limits of the earth to the vastness of the universe. The revelations of modern science, properly understood, are in no conflict with the religious truth that a Sovereign, Fatherly God is behind it all. Nor is it possible to interpret aright our own life, our coming into this world, and whatever powers and talents we possess, and our departure from it, except in terms of the gift of God who has put all its meaning and purpose into our life.

But it is supremely in the matter of our salvation in Christ that the New Testament continually stresses the idea of gift. "I will give you"—these four straightforward words were always on Jesus' lips. His gifts are the Word of the Father, the living water, the true bread, His flesh to eat, His life for the world, His peace, His glory, His new commandment. All that refreshes, heals and delivers comes from God. It is by all that that we enter the Kingdom which also is a gift— "Fear not little flock, it is your Father's good pleasure to give you the Kingdom" (Luke 12, 32). "God so loved the world that He *gave* His only begotten Son" (John 3, 16). "Thanks be to God for his unspeakable gift" (2 Cor. 9, 15). In John 4, 10 salvation is "the gift of God", and "the heavenly gift" in Heb. 6, 4. Such passages as Romans 3, 20–4, 8 and Ephes. 2, 1–10 deserve the closest attention. In them Paul is saying precisely the opposite of what he believed and strove for before his conversion, and the very thing that he so fiercely persecuted the early Christians for holding so bravely as they did. He now sees that the source of all salvation is the free goodness and the unmerited love of God. The self-righteous outlook and temper thwart and frustrate God's saving purpose; and so man is left with nothing in which to boast.

None of the gifts and blessings of God can be thrust upon unbelieving people—"they cannot enter in because of unbelief" (Hebrews 3, 19). But faith itself is a gift, for He seeks us first and moves us towards trust. Faith has been compared to a suspension-bridge flung across the chasm between God and man, but it is flung from the Divine side. In Romans 5, 15–21, in the contrast between the two Adams, forgiveness is "a free gift". The Holy Spirit which helps us to receive and respond to that gift is also a gift—John 7, 39; Acts 2, 38; 8, 15; 10, 45; 11, 17. Finally, eternal life is a gift—John 10, 28; 17, 2–3; Romans 6, 23; 1 John 5, 11. While sin gets wages, the wages of death, eternal life is not wages for anything. The devil pays wages, often very high; but God gives gifts in amazing generosity. The death which is the wages of sin is "the second death" (Rev. 2, 11; 20, 6, 14, 15; 21, 8). This is not the death of the body which comes to all alike, but the death of the soul. This awesome prospect, with other New Testament passages of the same kind, have received two different interpretations all down the generations. Some believe it to mean everlasting torment and some believe that it means eventual annihilation. It is hardly possible to maintain from either standpoint that the New Testament clearly means the one and not the other. The view of this matter which is taken usually depends on the type of theological approach which people have to the Gospel. What can certainly be said is that, for a being made in the image of God, nothing can be more dreadful than to separate himself from God.

The demand which arises out of the offer of the Gospel is one more example of the true unity of the Bible, for the necessity for law and obedience runs through all the Scriptures. The mother of Jesus Christ stated it perfectly for all true disciples "Whatsoever He saith unto you, do it" (John 2, 5). On the last night of His earthly life, in circumstances when everything had to be excluded except the utterly important, the word "command" is repeatedly heard—"Ye are my friends, if ye do whatsoever I command you"; these things I command you that ye love one another" (John 15, 14–17). A man's life is utterly changed by obedience to the heavenly vision (Acts 26, 19). One of the most tremendous things said in the New Testament is that even the Son has to learn obedience by the things which He suffered (Heb. 5, 8). The most characteristic form of Christian obedience is that which involves suffering for the servant as it did for the Master. When Christ calls upon us to take up our Cross and follow Him, that cross is not just our share in the inescapable trial and misfortune of the world, but the costly self-denial which we lay upon ourselves and willingly accept because our allegiance to Him is put above all else.

6

It remains now to consider what is the proper response of man to the full Gospel. The response begins and continues in personal, willing surrender, initiating a process of obedience as of a son not a slave (Gal. 4, 4–7). However reluctant they may be to acknowledge it, all men need to cry "What must I do to be saved?" and there is no true answer but one, "Believe on the Lord Jesus Christ and thou shalt be saved" (Acts 16, 30–31). It is well within man's own power to change his ideas, his views, his outward habits even, but not his inward self, his very nature. Such a renewal as that is possible only by securing a personal hold on the power which resides in the deliverance accomplished for all men by Christ, and by the actual experience of personal friendship with a Living Lord. In the words of J. H. Newman, "Christ died to purchase what He rose again to apply".

Growth in the Christian life is sustained in this way. The old man is put off and the new man is put on (Ephes. 4, 17–32); and we may now walk in newness of life (Romans 6, 4). The whole process by which Christ makes life new may be set forth in stages in His own words—"Come unto Me; Follow Me; Abide in Me; Go ye". In this way we become recognisably Christian. The title "Christian" was first applied to the followers of the Risen Christ at Antioch (Acts 11, 26), probably in scorn. But the name at its best implied from the start that these were people who had accepted certain beliefs from Him and were demonstrating them in characteristic action. The right belief and the appropriate action can never be separated, for they are joined together by God. There is no such thing as "the essential core of Christianity" in practice apart from the supporting belief. Christianity is first of all a *being* something in relation to God, and then a *doing* something before God and men. A kind of diffused Christianity which is primarily a system of conduct, to which the basic beliefs may be almost irrelevant and unnecessary, is far removed from the New Testament. But, for all who accept the basic beliefs, being a Christian is, as at Antioch, the living of a distinctive life which requires an explanation and which indeed needs the whole Gospel to explain it. It also involves the kind of life which reminds others of Jesus Christ, and encourages others to believe in Him.

The enterprise and the warfare of the Christian life lies in the effort to make our ideals actual. The dynamic for this lifelong task is our perception of the Love of God in Christ. To our continual astonishment, we have to remember that God loves us more than we love Him, more than we love our dearest, as much as He loves His Son and as much as the Cross cost Him. Only thus does power enter our life— "We are strengthened with might by His Spirit in the inner man, rooted and grounded in love" (Ephes. 3, 16–19). For the good life Christ is absolutely indispensable. "Without Me ye can do nothing" (John 15, 5); "I can do all things through Christ who strengtheneth me" (Phil. 4, 13). The Father is glorified as we bear much fruit (John 15, 8); and as time proceeds all the "fruits of the Spirit" appear, as we live and walk in the Spirit (Gal. 5, 22–26). Though we are not *saved* by our "fruits", we must be *known* by our fruits (Matt, 7, 15–20); and it is also by our works done in the body that we are to be judged (Matt. 16, 27; 2 Cor. 5, 10; Rev. 20, 12). It has been said that the devil has tried two ways of getting rid of Jesus Christ—first by putting Him on a Cross and then, when that failed, by putting Him on a pedestal. The only way to keep Him off the pedestal is to take Him with us into the rough, toilsome, militant world of action.

The saved life ought to be the spacious, abundant life; and we can best see what that implies in distinctive action by reference to some of Christ's most startling words. The finest story in the New Testament is in Mark 14, 1–9. This woman's action and the light it sheds on her character and on the character of the Gospel, have a signal honour paid to them by Christ which He gave to no other incident in His whole career. "Verily I say unto you, wheresoever the Gospel shall be preached throughout the whole world, this also that she hath done shall be spoken of for a memorial of her". Christ canonized and immortalized this woman on the spot. The two reasons for this amazing tribute are that her action was almost a perfect picture of His own approaching sacrifice, and a perfect picture of what all His followers should be. His death, like her deed, was inspired wholly by love, by very costly and lavish love. In her deed also we trace what He expects of all Christians—deep, personal attachment to Himself, original and daring action, action done at the right time and not too little and too late, and action which represents the very best possible in the circumstances. Along such lines as these the Gospel never ceases to challenge men.

Closely akin to this in demand is Christ's definition of true greatness—"Whosoever shall be great among you shall be your servant, and whosoever of you shall be chiefest shall be servant of all" (Mark 10, 42–45); and again He associates this with His own death by which He performed the supreme service for men in providing a ransom which is a means of pardon and deliverance. This view of greatness is the precise opposite of the worldly view, and so this is indeed one of His utterances that would turn the world upside down. H. G. Wells declared that the man who said this was standing on his head. To be served by other people, to be worked for by other people, is a poor thing compared with its opposite. In His Kingdom mere ambition has no place, for it is an order in which people are called to expend themselves to the full and not to be deterred by considerations of who gets the credit. Such a spirit of service needs steady sustenance, through prayer, worship and personal communion.

It is a very striking fact that there is only one saying of Jesus Christ which is reported six times in the Gospels, in slightly different forms. Most of His great words appear only once, and very few as often as three or four times. This word must have so impressed those who heard it that they could never get it out of mind—"He that loveth his life shall lose it and he that loseth his life for my sake and the gospel's shall find it" (Mark 8, 35; Matt. 10, 39; Matt. 16, 25; Luke 9, 24; Luke 17, 33; John 12, 25). The same idea is contained in passages like Mark 13, 13; Acts 20, 24; 1 Peter 4, 12–16; Phil. 3, 10; 2 Cor. 1, 5; 1 Cor. 12, 26; 1 Peter 5, 1; 1 John 4, 11; Heb. 13, 16; Romans 8, 10, 17; Col. 1, 24. It is not possible for the self-centred person to attain spiritual maturity. Self-centredness is ultimate self-stultification, as all sin is, and leads to boredom, futility, frustration, and low, cynical judgments of other people. Given time, Christ's way of life proves itself right and satisfying.

Christ does not present His demand for obedience in the form of a detailed set of rules and regulations. If He had done so, they would soon have passed out of date; and it is fairly easy to find ways of getting round rules and regulations. So He sets before us the perpetual challenge of a great principle, which is far harder to escape from. It is the principle of Love —"Lovest thou me?"—and it provides a new centre for living. In the Old Testament, the high water mark of its teaching on behaviour is found in passages like Micah 6, 8 and in "Love the Lord thy God and thy neighbour as thyself" (Deut. 6, 5; Lev. 19, 18; Luke 10, 25–27). The words just quoted, however high their standard, are not (as they are often mistakenly described) the Lord's new commandment, which is higher still, "Love as I have loved you" (John 13, 34; 15, 12; cf. John 3, 14–15; 4, 20). In Dr. William Temple's words, "The new commandment . . . is the impossible thing, except so far as we are 'in Christ', . . . as the branches are in the vine" (John 15, 5–12). But the old commandment is not superseded. It 'stands as a universal, and universally neglected, requirement; the new commandment . . . has a narrower range and an intenser quality. When the Church keeps the New Commandment, the world may keep the Old'.*

A specially important word of the Risen Lord is conveyed to us by Paul in his defence before King Agrippa. Had Paul not reported that the Risen Lord said this to him at his conversion on the Damascus road, we would have missed the best definition of the Christian mission and of the effects and benefits of the Gospel that we have in the whole New Testament. "I send you to open their eyes, to turn them from darkness unto light, and from the power of Satan unto God, that they may receive forgiveness, and an inheritance among those who are sanctified by the faith that is in me" (Acts 26, 17–18). This is a fuller Gospel than He had proclaimed in Galilee or Jerusalem, for now it is stated after the Cross, Resurrection and Ascension have actually happened. Paul knew well what it is to be blind and how hard it is to get people to realise and confess it. Christ opens our eyes to the truth about ourselves and God and to a whole world of light, goodness and power. But it is not enough to have the eyes opened. It is all too possible to see the right road and not take it. There is no necessity at all in "loving the highest when we

* *Readings in St. John's Gospel*, p.223.

see it", and so the turning from darkness unto light is required. Often indeed a sharper, more difficult turning is necessary. The power of evil can become very deeply entrenched in life, till it amounts to a fast bondage in the grip of Satan. Then comes the gift of forgiveness, frequently after a period of strain and trouble and battle, before we are willing to be reconciled to a God who is always friendly to us and loves us even when our back is turned against Him. And so finally we come to our inheritance—a consecrated life with meanings for here and now and greater meanings for the hereafter, in the inheritance of the saints in light in the Kingdom of His dear Son (Col. 1, 12–14). In this word of the Risen Christ, the Christian life is portrayed as ever moving upwards, the situation improving at every stage. The parable of the younger son may well be interpreted as a close parallel to this passage. He came to himself, i.e. his eyes were opened. He said "I will arise and go to my father", i.e. he was turned from darkness to light. He arose and went, i.e. he was turned from the power of Satan unto God. His father saw him, and had compassion and ran to meet him, i.e. that he may receive forgiveness. The best robe was brought out, i.e. he received his inheritance

It is not possible to be a Christian on our own. There is no such person in the New Testament as a Christian in isolation from the fellowship of believers which is the Church. Jesus Christ did not envisage a Churchless Christianity. "I will build my Church", He said—that was His fixed intention. The Church which He purposed is to be a perpetual memorial and challenge. It is built upon truth, the truth as it is in Christ, not upon our ideas of life and God. It is constructed out of living stones, lives being made new by Him. It is held together by the cement of love, and so it ought to be a very uncomfortable place for the unloving. Its chief corner stone is the Lord Himself. Paul does not hesitate to link Christ and the Church in the closest possible union—"I speak concerning Christ and the Church" (Ephes. 5, 32). The Church has no other purposes than the purposes of Christ.

"Christ also loved the Church and gave Himself for it" (Ephes. 5, 25). There is probably only one rule in life to which there can be no exception—if we disagree with Christ, stand on the other side from Him, and lightly value what He esteems highly, we are bound to be utterly wrong, for He must always be right. If we do not love the Church and sacrifice for it, we separate ourselves from Him, for He did both. Membership in the Church, the body of Christ, is not a loose, social relationship, but a close, organic relationship (Romans 12, 4–5). Within the body of Christ, Christians have to encourage and strengthen each other, submit to the direction and control of the Head, and resolve that all atomistic, unbiblical individualism has to be given up, since there can be no true life outside the body. If someone outside the Church should pronounce that the Church is dead, there is no reason why they should contradict that by keeping up the attack on the Church. They will discover that it is impossible to get the supposed corpse out of the way. If people inside the Church say such a thing, it is a confession that they are dead themselves. "The gates of hell shall not prevail against it". These very daring words signify three closely-related ideas. The powers of wickedness can greatly harm the Church, but they will be defeated. It is the Church's business to sally out and attack the strongholds of evil and break down their gates. Since the word "hades" normally means the abode of death, it is a sound exegesis which says that the Church will never pass through the gates of death. The Church, like the Word of God, is "an anvil which has broken many hammers". While the world's life lasts, there will be a Church to make known the full Gospel.

Accordingly, a proper response to the demand of the Gospel is an active share in the Church's missionary task. The Gospel for all the world is not the recumbent Buddha nor Mohammed with the sword, but the Christ of the Cross and the empty Tomb. "As the Father hath sent me, even so send I you" (John 17, 18; 20, 21). The Christian mission has its origin in heaven. In its movement it is a Divine "down and out"—down from above, and then out to the uttermost part of the earth (Acts 1, 8). The true furnishings of the Holy Table, it has been well said, are bread and wine, the Bible and a globe. Because the Lord hath spoken, because the love of Christ constrains us, there is a Divine "must" laid upon the Church; and the sure way for the Church to lose the good gift from above is to refuse to share it.

Finally, it is the Gospel of eternal life. "This is life eternal that they might know thee, the only true God, and Jesus Christ whom thou hast sent" (John 17, 3). "Eye hath not seen nor ear heard, neither have entered into the heart of man, the things which God hath prepared for them that love Him" (1 Cor. 2, 9). To human beings who have no hold on immortality by nature, the Gospel offers new life from the dead. We are "born anew to a living hope through the resurrection of Jesus Christ from the dead" (1 Peter 1, 3). Without this hope, all is vain, says Paul (1 Cor. 15, 14–20, 35–58). The Christian is granted both an immediate experience and an assured expectation of eternal life. We enter the kingdom now by faith, we become converted and become as children, and we find new riches in our poverty because He made Himself poor for us (2 Cor. 8, 9). God wants to have us with him forever. For that He gave us life itself and the foretaste of the heavenly life, and He so looks forward to our coming that He prepares for it in a magnificent, inconceivable, indescribable way. To those who love Him, He offers "all this—and Heaven too". There is no boundary to the unsearchable riches of Christ.

It may be confidently claimed that there is deep agreement on these essentials of the full Gospel throughout the whole Church. That oneness in Christ, it has to be gratefully acknowledged, is not something for which we have to strive and argue, for it is an experienced fact. Whatever divisions there are on aspects of the doctrine of the Church, its ministry and sacraments, that is not so hopeless a situation as radical divergence on the Gospel itself would be. There are also deep disagreements on the further issues which arise in all the next chapters, and they must be faced. But the Church has a full-time task in proclaiming the full Gospel, aggressively and triumphantly, so that men may marvel at the wonderful works of God.

CHAPTER TWO

Hindrances to Evangelism

THERE are two predictions which can be made with reasonable confidence at the present stage in human affairs. One concerns the world as a whole, and the other the Christian religion; and they are closely, if not inextricably, related.

The world cannot remain much longer poised in the present state of tension and peril. Among the possibilities are two which are exceedingly dark. An outbreak of war on a world scale, with modern weapons, would bring an unimaginable orgy and holocaust of mutual destruction. So we are warned by the most responsible statesmen and scientists. It would appear to be only too true that on the human side nothing is holding back this catastrophe except a universal fear of all that it would involve. But the Christian believes that the restraint of God's pity and patience is also a supreme factor. The other menacing possibility is a rapid and widespread extension of materialistic Communism, without resort to large-scale war. If this took place, it would most likely be in the areas where immense and growing populations are undeveloped, illiterate and underfed. It must never be forgotten that the majority of the human race are still at the stage when they are prepared to pay almost any price for economic uplift and to sacrifice all the other freedoms for the promise of economic freedom. The rest of the world tends to ignore, to its own great danger, the fact that the peoples which have already in the last half century gone Communist were destitute and illiterate when they accepted that system. If, as the experts tell us, two thirds of the human race is hungry, and if only five per cent of the people in the non-Christian world can read or write, the challenge is formidable.

What are the prospects for the Christian religion in such a world as this? Obviously it is facing a threat as great as it has ever known, and yet it may be predicted that the chances of a reawakening of the Christian forces are better for the second half of the twentieth century than they have been since the middle ages. In an ultimate sense revival comes through the unforseeable and unpredictable operation of the Holy Spirit, but we may abide by that steadfast anchor of faith and hope while we also make as searching and reverent a diagnosis of the contemporary situation as we can.

There is little wisdom in judgments which are too immediate and short-term. It is a longer look backward and forward that is likely to be helpful and stimulating. Looking to the next half century, it can surely be said that the Christian Church is either to be pushed out to the circumference of things more than it now is, with the big tides of the world's life sweeping past it, or it is to experience a rebirth which will bring it again to the very centre of life in all its manifold forms. Such a rebirth is bound to be shaking and shattering, as Amos, the first of the great prophets, said the "day of the Lord" would be (Amos 5, 18–20)—and we must not let that slip out of mind when we pray for revival.

An essential condition for revival, so far as we can see from the human side, our only point of vision, is that the Church should take stock of and take the true measure of the forces which in the last century have peculiarly contributed to the undermining of Christianity, and of the hindrances which hold back Christianity in every generation. It is an interesting and significant fact that it was in the one great period in this country when Church attendance was at its best that the forces were beginning to function powerfully which have made the entire scene of Christian witness more difficult. That one period was the second half of the nine-teenth century, the renowned Victorian age. The habit of Church-going was more general then than at any other period, with the one exception of the industrial workers in the fast-growing towns. But all the time there were taking place such far-reaching movements as the rise of modern science and psychology, the swift tendencies towards a wholly materialist view of history and society, and the disturbance occasioned inside and outside the Church by Biblical criticism. Without exception, these have turned out to be influences raising the largest possible problems for the Church. The time has come for the Church to make an honest and, if necessary, "agonizing re-appraisal" of them all, to show the world that it welcomes whatever is good and true in them, and that it realises to the full what it was that even the materialistic social movements were blunderingly seeking to emphasize and secure.

The Church has no interest whatever in appearing suspicious of the scientific method, scientific research, and the gains of scientific invention. Truth never contradicts truth, from whatever source it comes. To the Christian mind all facts are facts of God, and are only facts because He has made them so. It would be a grievous tragedy indeed if the spirit of reverent enquiry were to be found in science and not in religion. In the early stages, a century ago, conflict was almost inevitable and blame lay heavily on both parties. The first impression made by the work of Darwin was that it dispensed with God, and he sadly confessed in his "Auto-biography" that his researches had blunted and atrophied his earlier artistic and religious susceptibilities, even to the point of extinction. Some of those who carried on his work went even further, and in the wrong hands scientific progress can be most dangerous. As a recent estimate of Darwin says "The breach that opened in 1860 between religion and Darwinism was the greatest intellectual disaster of the 19th century. When the Church of Theology was ready for a truce, the Church of Science sharpened its weapons".

Science has its own big problems to face, and in not a few scientific quarters there is a welcome sense of alarm as to the practical applications of scientific knowledge, and a ready acknowledgment that, without Christian belief and the principles of behaviour that flow from it, the application of science could be ruinous. The Church must not suggest that people have to give up their science in order to be Christian. All that a scientist holds true as a scientist can and ought to be retained, along with a full allegiance to the eternal truth of the Gospel. The man who is able to effect in his own soul that happy alliance will not be deficient in the fear of God nor in the healthy concern as to where science may lead an unbelieving world. The Church can rejoice in the marvels of science and yet wholeheartedly claim that the marvels of the Christian interpretation of the universe and of life, of faith and of prayer are greater still.

2

The Church, facing this troubled and anxious future, has no more urgent task before it than to assert in unequivocal terms the authority of the Bible, the wholly sufficient instrument which God has put into the Church's hands for the fulfilment of its mission. This is not to be done by any harking back to old positions which had grown up in rigid forms before the storm of "Biblical criticism" broke. The Bible does not need the buttress of any mechanical theory of verbal inerrancy, helped out at difficult points by some sort of allegorical method of interpretation. There is a sounder attitude to the problem, which gives us a richer and more wonderful Bible, a Bible which is utterly unique and indispensable and irreplaceable for its great purpose of bringing the soul of man to God, a Bible in which God speaks to men as

47

He does nowhere else and says such things as only God can say, a Bible the whole truth of which has to be conveyed and interpreted by the Church to the whole world.

It is not to be denied but to be deplored that the Bible has suffered at the hands of a certain type of scholar. From time to time, a brilliant expert appears who concentrates all his energy on the analysis of some selected part of the Bible, without having much knowledge of or concern for the Bible as a whole. If such a scholar is not committed to the tremendous themes of the Bible and is detached from the life of the Church and outside its worship and service, what he says on his special subject may be wholly unbalanced, and consequently disturbing to many. There are other scholars whose researches have led them to question the once-for-all supernatural character of the contents of the Bible and who strive hard to pare down its truth to the limits and levels of man's unaided reason.

For such reasons there has been for a long time a dark suspicion that the authority of the Bible has been destroyed, that it can no longer be trusted and that it has to be relegated to the museum along with other discarded relics of myth and legend. Far from this being so, the truth is that the Bible documents have been sifted more searchingly than any other documents in the world, and their essential truth and character triumphantly vindicated. As the assured foundation of the Christian religion its trustworthiness is impregnably established. True scholarship is no enemy of the word of God. The best Biblical scholars have not been irreverent, godless men, bent on tearing the Bible to pieces. They have usually been most orthodox and conservative in theological belief, and devout and sincere in personal faith. Their work must not be hampered. The questions that engage their attention are important, but secondary, such as the date, the authorship, the sources and the structure of the various books of the Bible. All this is of the highest value as we probe deep into the vital truth of the Scriptures and as we discover that it is the Bible which judges us, not we the Bible.

While it is probably true that it is easier to demolish an inadequate and false doctrine of the authority and inspiration of the Bible than to build up and state clearly a satisfactory and true doctrine, the Church must not shirk the task for the sake of the revival we hope and pray for.

In pursuing this task, the Church will be able to show why we must have the Old Testament as well as the New, what are the deep reasons which make both to be Christian Scriptures, how the unity of the Bible is in Christ alone, and why it is all required for our grasp of the full and final Gospel. It is along such lines as these that we penetrate into the true meaning of the claim made in 2 Timothy 3, 16—"All scripture is given by inspiration of God, and is profitable for doctrine, for reproof, for correction, for instruction in righteousness". The writers of the books of the Bible, living at very different times, facing very different situations, and using very different literary forms, were inspired by God in the deepest and surest of all ways. God had made His approach to them, conveyed His mind to them in their private experience and their reflection upon the scene all around them, guided their thoughts, strengthened them for action, led them to see the meaning of events, unfolded to them His purpose, and assisted them as they sought to give expression to all this in words. Such inspiration comes, as it usually does, in the toil and striving of life. There is nothing mechanical about it, it is all dynamic; and the men so inspired are never more free than when they yield to the Divine impulse.

It would be a great gain if those who are separated by different views of inspiration could realise and demonstrate how much they are truly one in their acceptance of the final supremacy of the Word of God. There are few nowadays to defend the "dictation" view of inspiration. In the year 1860, in the midst of the bitter controversies occasioned by the theory of evolution, Dean Burgon, preaching from the University pulpit at Oxford, expressed it thus—"Every book of it, every chapter of it, every verse of it, every word of it, every syllable of it (where are we to stop?), every letter of it, is the direct utterance of the Most High". Dr. Packer, in a recent book "Fundamentalism and the Word of God", says that "this is nothing more than a rhetorical affirmation of the divine origin of all Scripture. Burgon is affirming the fact of inspiration: he is not discussing the mode of it, and the passage contains not a word to suggest that dictation was the method whereby Scripture was given". If that is what the Dean had in mind, it can only be said that there was little inspiration in the very misleading words he chose to express it. But it is a relief to know that he also wrote "Let me not be told that this is to advocate a mechanical theory. The method of inspiration is one of the many things I cannot fully understand, much less pretend to explain".

Further, it would be a great gain if the advocates of complete verbal inerrancy could understand that there is nothing of value to be lost by giving up the form of that doctrine in which it is now commonly stated. Everyone agrees that there are considerable verbal differences in the various manuscripts of the books of the Bible, that these manuscripts are all copies separated from the originals by a long stretch of time, that the Bible has yielded itself to a wonderful degree to translation into a thousand tongues, and that it is one or other of the translations that most people use and are able to use. But, while all this is accepted, it is also claimed that verbal infallibility belongs to the Scriptures *as originally given*". In other words, if we could get back to the autographs of the books, we would have the authentic, verbally-perfect Word of God. But, so far as is known, the autograph of every book of the Bible has disappeared, beyond all reasonable hope of recovery; and God apparently did not judge it necessary to preserve the manuscripts in their original form. The words "as originally given" have the appearance of "an escape clause".

The Bible is the Word of God, because in the Bible alone we know how God has spoken and acted for the salvation of men, and it is the inner work of the Holy Spirit which makes us sure of this. What matters, therefore, is not precise verbal accuracy in a superficial, horizontal sense, but deep, vertical truth revealed for our eternal salvation, to be perceived by anyone who makes a reverent and obedient approach to the Scriptures. All this is mediated to us by the Bible writers who in their own personalities received the revelation in terms of their own day and generation, until the time when chosen men made their own encounter with the Word made Flesh.

The form in which "Biblical criticism" (an unfortunate term) broke upon the Church was indeed a shock; but we have had ample time now to recover from that shock. If tensions in this field are growing, not decreasing, that is bound to be a severe handicap in modern evangelism. It is almost certain that there will always be conservative and less conservative approaches to this question. But this must not be allowed to obscure the quintessential Either-Or of the Bible. "Either the Bible is a book under our control, it is a book among other books, it propounds a religion among other religions, it offers a jumble of wisdom among a host of other wisdoms—or the Bible is the account of a happening, *the* happening, *the* key to man's existence and history, the account of the ways of God with men, a God who goes particular ways at particular times. Then it controls us and all our theological thinking". (W. Pelz, Irreligious Reflections on the Christian Church, page 22.) Is it not a false antithesis which prevents those who hold different views of inspiration from joining hands in the recognition that the authority of the Bible cannot be separated from its inspiration, but that inspiration is a bigger concept than any theory of the method of inspiration?

3

The most formidable obstacle to the Gospel is the radical, age-long opposition of human nature to the Gospel. It is equally true that human nature deeply craves for the satisfaction which only the Gospel can supply. This is a great paradox, and there is no deeper contradiction at the heart of life. Evangelism has always to take account of the stubborn fact that this is the very constitution of human beings. It is idle to speculate on whether there is more sin in the world than there used to be. The answer to that question will probably vary with the age of the person who makes the judgment. Of course, there are more sinners in the world because there are more people, and also the power at man's disposal has increased to a dangerous degree. But the unchanging fact is that, on one side of his being, man resists the near approach and control of God, even though he defeats and destroys himself in so doing. It is in that sense that Paul's words are true, "There is no difference, for all have sinned and come short of the glory of God" (Romans 3, 22–23).

The theological issue here is the doctrine of man and the soul. The ancient idea of "the soul naturally Christian" is at best a one-sided statement. Doubtless the doctrine of man's total depravity is also one-sided, if it means that there is nothing but evil in man, whereas it should only mean that evil has infected every aspect of man's being. To all the more optimistic views of human nature, we may find a corrective, set forth perhaps in extreme terms, in the prayer of William Drummond of Hawthornden—

> "Grant when at last the spirit shall leave this tomb,
> This loathsome shop of sin, this mansion blind,
> And called before the royal seat doth come,
> It may a Saviour, not a Judge, there find."

There ought to be ready, generous acknowledgment of the good in ordinary human beings. There is plenty evidence of courage, kindness, courtesy and unselfishness in the human situation; and especially in times of emergency these qualities seem almost to take command. All this must be a pleasure to God, and indeed it has its source in God, a God who has "no pleasure in the death of the wicked, but that he may turn from his ways and live" (Ezekiel 18, 23). So all who present the Gospel and represent the Church to other people have first of all to love them and show how deeply they care for them. Whenever people suspect that those who approach them in the name of Christ do not really love or care for them, all influence for good is at an end. The Christian has always to be one who comes as a beggar, telling other beggars where good food is to be found. The Gospel is bound to be resisted when it is set forth in merely argumentative, denunciatory ways. Even in evangelism there can appear a proud, hectoring pomposity which is fatal.

Nevertheless there is a dreadful solidarity of all mankind in sin. This something in man which God cannot countenance, which is utterly repulsive to God, is the tragedy of all the ages. Human nature is a strange mixture, for it is capable of terrible things and marvellous things. The same man who can "glory in the Cross" (Gal. 6, 14) can also "glory in his shame" (Phil. 3, 19). There indeed is man's highest and his lowest—the highest to which he can rise, the lowest to which he can fall. When we remember the big strains that modern civilization and the general state of the world place on the moral fibre of human beings, bigger than at any time since man emerged out of primitive barbarism, we should be patient and understanding in our judgments, especially of the young generation who have never known a world other than this present one, who are not responsible for the state of the world which they inherited from their forebears, a world in which firm, ethical principle counts for little. To that kind of world, the Church has to proclaim that the natural man cannot know the things of God (1 Cor. 2, 14–

16). On the unspiritual side of his nature, man loves the world more than he loves God. As a result he has little compelling sense of the supernatural. His horizon tends to become bounded by the things of this life, and his main tests of everything are material. Until his eyes are opened, he cannot even see the kingdom of God, far less enter it, and he has no equipment to judge the things of God. The battle of the Gospel is always against all that formidable resistance, but it is a subduing and exhilarating fact that the Gospel is breaking down that resistance in some people every day.

Paul uses exceedingly strong words in Romans 3, 4—"we make Him a liar". It is closely paralleled in 1 John 1, 10: 5, 10 "If we say we have not sinned, we make him a liar, and his word is not in us". "He that believeth on the Son of God hath the witness in himself: he that believeth not God hath made him a liar; because he believeth not the record that God gave of his Son". By denying our sin, by denying what God has done in His Son, we make Him a liar; but the passage in Romans 3, 4 suggests that the oldest and biggest lie of all is to treat the unseen and the spiritual as unreal, untrue, or irrelevant. This attitude which makes the whole Bible to be basically false is a continual temptation to the natural man. The modern world encourages at every point the worship of success, and relies too much on the assumption that it is not likely that people will consent to do or sacrifice much without some obvious incentive—very much in the manner of the schoolboy who asked "But what exactly did Stephen get out of being stoned?" The Bible has a wholly healthy attitude to the material, calls on men to glorify God in the use of the material, and yet unweariedly warns men not to worship it.

The warfare of the Gospel is against the whole realm of evil, which has its own subtle strategy, and its periods of advance and retreat. It is against that realm that we are called to put on "the whole armour of God, for we wrestle not against flesh and blood, but against principalities and powers, against the rulers of the darkness of this world, against spiritual wickedness in high places" (Ephes. 6, 11–12). All who witness to the Gospel have to face forward in this battle, and not to turn and run, for there is no armour for the back in Paul's definition of the panoply of God. The greatest of all errors is to underestimate the powers of evil, and Paul is not overestimating them here. There is no book in the New Testament where the realm of evil does not stand out in prominence. The very purpose for which Jesus was manifested is to destroy the works of the devil (1 John 3, 8).

"A great and effectual door is opened to me, and there are many adversaries" (1 Cor. 16, 9). There have been great advances of the Gospel, but always in face of powerful opposition. The message of the Kingdom has been welcomed and fought against, loved and hated. It is the only force in the world that offers nothing but good to men, and yet the good it offers is not wanted, or at least not eagerly enough wanted, or not wanted on God's terms. The Gospel emphasis that the full meaning of life is not to be found within itself, but comes to it from outside and from above is resisted by man in many of his moods and assumptions. He is not willing to admit that he tends to be bad, to be given to self-love and self-will, unless he is corrected and changed. It is much too easy an explanation of the slow advance of Christianity to lay the main responsibility for it at the door of the Church, however grievous its weaknesses and betrayals; it is mainly due to dislike of what Christ stands for. But we have not to be terrified by that foremost adversary, or by any other (Phil. 1, 28; Heb. 10, 27; Luke 13, 17; 21, 15). This hour, as every hour, is one to challenge the world. Two features of life cannot be overlooked as the challenge is made. First, there is a distinct tendency in people towards loss of personal, spiritual fervour, as their outward circumstances improve. This is the insidious danger of materialism. With better standards of living and increased comfort, there is a disposition to forget that man's life does not consist in the abundance of the things which he possesses. This has long been a danger in the older Churches, but it is now appearing in the younger too. Times of material prosperity are not generally times of revival, when people turn in penitence and faith to God. There is a truly Christian attitude to "getting on", and people need to be continually reminded of it.

Secondly, in this world of expanding education, the radical opposition of human nature to the Gospel is accentuated. This does not mean that it is better to leave people ignorant, as if ignorance and religion were true bedfellows. Education tends to become more and more specialized, and this is indeed a crisis at the University level. It is all too easy to go through a course of advanced education without learning from it anything at all of what life itself is, and what is its meaning and purpose; and for some that is darkly obscured by their higher education. It is not the obvious purpose of education to help people to "see life large and see it whole". But that is precisely the function of religion, and pre-eminently of Christianity, on the basis of its special revelation. Of course, many highly-educated people, including foremost scientists, are devout Christians and, on the contrary, many simple people of little education are "far ben" in the affairs of the soul. Education can be a great blessing, but it is no substitute for Christ.

4

Another hindrance to the Gospel is the wide gap between faith and action. This is all pervasive and exceedingly damaging. "What do ye more than others?" is the question of Jesus Christ to His disciples. It plainly means that His followers can come to be too like other people, so that there is little obvious difference between the Churchgoer's way of living and the non-Churchgoer's, especially in countries where a kind of general Christian background has been provided by centuries of Christian teaching. The standard set by Paul is one short of which too many fall—"Ye are our epistles, written in our hearts, known and read of all men" (2 Cor. 3, 2). It is certain that Christianity is a very definite and a very exacting creed, and it is most misleading to the world to convey the impression that in actual life it is scarcely distinguishable from normal, decent, worldly life. No injustice is done by saying that many Church people know more of how to get on in this world than of how to lay hold on eternal life, and that not a few people in Church are as anxious, fretful and self-seeking as some outside.

To say such things does not imply that there has been in recent times a serious collapse in standards of Christian living, for this covers every period of Christian history. Still less has it anything to do with the heresy of salvation through good works. There is no tampering here with the Scriptural doctrine of justification by faith alone, and no lifting of the fundamental divine-human relationship out of the realm of God's grace. These are the very roots of the Christian life, but from these roots there should grow manifest fruits (Matt. 7, 20). Where there is no root, there will be no fruit. The inwardness of Christian experience—"rooted and grounded in love"—is of the very first moment, and without it there can be no true outwardness. The fruit corresponds to the root, and proclaims what the root is. The fruit grows slowly, but we have to see that at the root there is a well (cf. Joseph, Genesis 49, 22). Whatever is fruitful of good is true. This is the principle by which to test the truth of rival religions and philosophies of life, the value of any Christian revival, the benefits of acts and exercises of worship, and the honesty of a personal confession.

A large part of the radical opposition to the Gospel in the realm of action is in conflict with the pattern of obedience which the Gospel provides and insists upon. In this sense too the word has to be made flesh. But it is a puzzling phenomenon that there are Christians who would be as much shocked by the enthusiastic practice of Christianity in outward life as by the outright denial of its basic doctrines. In recent years, a good number of groups have been assembled under the title "Study Fellowship for Christian Action", and the slogan was "See, judge, act". As time has passed, they have tended to become just "Study fellowships" and the "Christian action" has been quietly dropped. They have found that it is easier to see than to judge and that to act is hardest of all.

When Spurgeon heard the gibe that "it takes four million sermons a year to keep our England up to the mark", he is alleged to have said that the mark would have been lower without the sermons but that indeed it was not very high. A famous preacher of half a century ago used to chide his well-off congregation for crowding in to enjoy his sermons and then "tumble into their prayerless beds". It is not really of much benefit to say that kind of thing, if it becomes merely a pleasant topic of conversation, while the people continue the enjoying and the tumbling. Dr. T. R. Glover is reported as saying "When I hear about people being converted, I wish to ask how far has the angle turned". Does it turn far enough to take in the Sermon on the Mount. There, in Matthew 5 to 7, is a pattern of obedience, not for the multitude as a whole, but for the committed disciples, which, if more manifest, would give the whole Gospel a better chance. Christians tend to be too selective of the ethical responsibilities of their faith, and they have been specially neglectful of the Sermon on the Mount, the standards of which are embarrassingly high. A preacher once delivered a course of sermons on this part of Christ's teaching, under the title "Idealism in a hurry". Others have tried to get round it by describing it as "an impossible possibility", whatever that may be.

The area of living in which Christians generally show a quite distinctive difference from those who have made no such profession is small compared with the broad stretches of living in which both are firmly anchored, a conventional Christian morality which is itself the product of long centuries of diffused and at points diluted Christianity. It has to be stressed that the issue here is not between one Church against another, or one group of Christians against another; and no one is in a position to throw stones. Those who are nearest to the ideals would be the last to wish to throw stones. But there is ample room for the admission that, if more people who believe the Gospel thought less of laying up treasures upon earth and were more obviously turning the other cheek, going the second mile, loving and praying for their enemies, the Gospel itself would be more effectively commended and more widely accepted. The theological emphasis in evangelism is utterly important, but it can be made too prominent if thereby the action-emphasis is obscured or distorted. The Church can be paralyzed at the centre if we convey the impression that what was so costly to God can be easy for us.

An understandable but unreliable test of preaching is the size of the congregation. However desirable it is to get people in large numbers within the hearing of the Gospel, it is a radical mistake to judge that the Church is doing little or no business unless there are many people in attendance. Every generation has been marked by the unpalatable and mystifying fact that there is no necessary or manifest relationship between outstandingly good preaching and outstandingly Christian behaviour in the hearers. Some of the Christians of rarest quality seldom hear what is popularly understood to be a great or brilliant sermon.

The Gospel must always be preached as both comfort and challenge. In both directions its presentation can become lopsided, but usually it is by the lack of transforming challenge that the greater harm is done. Deeds are the best credentials of the Gospel. It is only by letting our light shine before men that they will be led to glorify God, after they have seen our good works (Matt. 5, 17); and it is only by outward obedience that we can "show forth the praises of Him who hath called us out of darkness into His marvellous light" (1 Peter 2, 6–9). There is no sure way of convincing an unbelieving world

that Christ died for all, except by no longer living unto ourselves (2 Cor. 5, 12–15). To be sure, the all-important thing
in preaching is the bread of the Gospel, not he who serves it;
but the world is likely to be most impressed by the results in
the life of those who receive the bread.

The good preacher is the one who leads people so near to
God that they will see for themselves the supremacy of
worship, and be present at it whether he is there or not. A
Church is not an assemblage of sermon-tasters, and it is too
much to suppose that popular judgment is really competent
to decide what fine preaching is. It can so easily happen that
preaching itself becomes one of the hindrances to the Gospel.
The effects which every sincere preacher covets are illumina-
tion of the dark mind, a changed outlook, a new depth of
living which ensures peace and poise in life, and a continual
increase of the outward fruits whichs are the increase of
faith and faithfulness. In her life of Charlotte Bronte, Mrs.
Gaskell describes the prevailing religion of the period as "not
working down into their lives and not meddling with them".
A Roman Cardinal, surveying the vast treasures of the Vati-
can, said to the Pope. "Past is the time when the Church can
say, Silver and gold have I none", and the Pope sadly re-
plied, "Past also is the time when we can say, Rise up and
walk". But that is always the best evidence, and it is not
secured merely when people enjoy a sermon, and still less
when they "simply revel" in the preacher.

The Church, by its preaching and pastoral ministry, has
in every generation produced splendid examples of what it
is to be a Christian. They are to be found in every class and
country—and they have the qualities which marked those
disciples who first of all at Antioch were called Christians
(Acts 11, 26)—their life a constant reminder to others of
Jesus Christ, their faith and conduct inspired by the conception of God's personal love for them as they had learned
it from Him, and engaged in a never-ceasing adventure of
advancing a cause, extending the Church and changing the
world. As yet, however, such Christians are not numerous

enough to make a sufficient impression on a world so sub-Christian or anti-Christian in its attitudes and standards. There was a time when preachers were described as "angels on Jacob's ladder, going up and down, down and up like anything"! In our time we probably do not have "great" preachers as in last century. God seems to have answered the prayer made last century—"make no more giants, Lord, but elevate the race". The general level of preaching is much higher than in the days when Church-going was an accepted convention—days which did not cover a long period.

What counts so much for the spread of the Gospel is the degree of response given by those who are hearing it. Gratitude lies at the very heart of the grace of the Gospel, and open, expressed, acted gratitude, one of the most attractive qualities of all, would help to impress and win many who are outside in the cold, bleak world of unbelief or uncertainty. Within the Christian fold there are not a few who follow all too faithfully the cynical exhortation of Ecclesiastes 7, 16, and they are not too obsessed with trying to be good, but are content with some kind of happy medium between being righteous overmuch and wicked overmuch. Others inside the Church hesitate in the sphere of action because inwardly they have refused the final, unshaken certainty which comes only by belief in God's special Revelation; they trust too much to intuition and it is hardly possible to be fully Christian by intuition.

There is little room to doubt that the majority of Church-goers do not sufficiently practise private religious habits, regular Bible reading and prayer; and so they are out of touch with the dynamic that translates faith into action. Since it is certain that Christians are "epistles known and read of all men", it is urgent that they should be "manifestly declared to be the epistle of Christ" (2 Cor. 3, 2–3). It is impossible to lift the general level of the Church's life above the personal life of its members. Nowadays it is true, as it has always been, that the finest types of character are nurtured within the Christian Church. But it is also true, in lands where there has been a tradition of Christian teaching for centuries, that there are many people outside the Church who compare favourably with many inside. There is much diffused Christianity in the background and environment of life, but that is no lasting safeguard for society, nor any guarantee that such Christianity will indefinitely survive. We have to welcome goodness of life, wherever it appears, for it is always derived from the Spirit of God, but this does not diminish the special responsibility which rests on those who hear the Gospel and profess to believe it. "Take heed how ye hear" (Luke 8, 18) is our Lord's striking word to us. There is an old saying that "he walks far who sees a word right home". Every word of the Gospel has to get home in outward as well as inward living. Men become hard of hearing, and listen to the Gospel in a detached, superficial, selective fashion rather than in the earnest, resolved, penitent and dedicated way that ensures that the word gets right home. The way to get the full benefit of the preached word is to go and act upon it. That is the continual responsibility of hearing. The prophet Ezekiel, like many another prophet in every age, was perplexed and saddened by the response to his preaching, "And, lo, thou art unto them as a very lovely song of one that hath a pleasant voice, and can play well on an instrument; for they hear thy words, but they do them not" (Ezekiel 33, 32). Responsible hearing involves a greatly increased sense that in all things and at all times we are "in our Great Taskmaster's eye", that we have a personal reliance on the comfort of God's promises, that we have a watchful eye on our own spiritual growth, our advance in sincerity, honesty, joy, kindness, and that we have a continual, vivid concern about the way other people live. In these ways we abide in Christ, "and he that saith he abideth in Him ought himself also to walk even as He walked" (1 John 2, 6). Consequently, the Gospel itself will have free course and be glorified.

5

To make known the Gospel to all men is a matter of life
and death for the Church, but the degree of lethargy within
the Church for its missionary task is a serious handicap to
the progress of the Gospel. This position must be held firmly
and penitently, after all allowance is made for very notable
advances which have been made and for the great increase
in informed and sacrificial missionary concern over the last
century and a half. "The Church has a history only because
God has given to it the privilege of participating in His own
mission". Can we get the truth of that judgment of Dr.
Wilhelm Andersen across to the rank and file of the
Churches, amid the swift movement of world events in our
time? The challenge of the present era to the missionary
spirit involves three tasks—to help people to see the actual
facts of the Christian situation all over the world with clarity
and urgency, to proclaim the elements of hope in the present
dark scene, without getting into the company of the prophets
of gloom and disaster in this shattered age, and to concentrate on the primary issue that the great majority of the
people of the world are as yet unevangelised and that the
Gospel has not yet in any effective sense been preached to
the multitudes. It is a miracle of God's mercy that He seems
to be laying on a spiritually-depleted Church a most heavy
burden. That may well be the measure of His amazing trust
in us. As at the beginning, great and effectual doors are still
open, and there are many adversaries. Christianity still has
the word to speak, if we can make it heard. If mankind is
to have a future, Christianity must be the dominant force
in that future. Even if worldwide catastrophe should befall,
Christianity will find a way of defying the darkness and
ruin and sending out its light again.

Fifty years ago Dr. P. T. Forsyth preached a very remarkable missionary sermon on the text "I, if I be lifted up from the earth will draw all men unto Me". A long quotation from it is in place here. "The great Charter of missions lies not in any express command of Christ. They would be just as binding on us if the command at the close of Matthew's Gospel had dropped off with the last page of the first manuscript. They would arise, as they did for Paul, not out of any injunction but out of the nature of Christ's Person and especially from His Cross, His Resurrection and His exalted life, judgment and reign. If they had not been commanded by Christ, they would have been invented by the Holy Spirit. The imperative of missions is in the Gospel rather than in the gospels, in the urgency of the Risen Christ than in the precept of the Christ on earth. So entirely are missions supernatural in their character that they must rise and fall with our faith in the supernatural. The mainspring of missions is not the judgment that *will* fall, but the judgment that *has fallen* in the Cross. It is not so much pity for perishing heathen, as faith and zeal for Christ's crown rights set up forever in the deed which is decisive for all the world. The world's awful need is less than Christ's awful victory. The width of the Gospel springs from its depths".

Can we get the impact of such a tremendous statement across to the people in the pew? Such a vision, and the compelling truth in such a vision, has not yet begun to glimmer in the consciousness and conscience of at least two thirds of the Church's membership. Even so, the missionary expansion of the Church in modern times, the emergence of the young Churches in all their appeal and encouragement, and the overflow of benefit and stimulus from them to the older Churches, are among the most significant and promising things of history. The Christian religion is indeed worldwide already. It is no longer a dream but a fact that the Christian faith can be planted in every soil, and that a fellowship can be brought together from people of every race, country, creed and tongue, held together by a central allegiance to Jesus Christ as Saviour and Lord.

An inescapable, imperative part of our response to the missionary challenge of our time is to arouse the people of the Churches to the totally new environment within which the spread of the unchanging Gospel has to be undertaken. The setting is one of unprecedented, revolutionary change, especially in the geographical areas where the greater part of missionary activity has to proceed. As a result of two world wars and also of other deep, irresistible movements over a longer period of history, this is "an hour big with destiny". Amid these vast upheavals and ceaseless ferments, the Church has to proclaim the Gospel to people who are painfully aware of the pressure on their lives of forces over which they have little control. Many new nations have come to the birth of political independence. The supremacy of the white race is at an end in Asia and is widely challenged in Africa. The old religions and cults have been experiencing a kind of revival, closely connected with the upsurge of nationalism. The civilization of the west which sent out Christianity at the great missionary epochs is discredited in the eyes of all these new peoples. In all the areas where missions have been at work there is the problem of rapidly increasing population with its growing pressure on the available means of subsistence. The revolution in literacy which is to put the ability to read into the hands of a thousand million people before the end of the century is a factor which has not yet been taken as seriously as it deserves by the missionary societies. It is reckoned that three fifths of the human race are outside the iron curtain, but they are mostly illiterate. Into that world, at almost every conceivable point, Communism has permeated itself, with discipline, enthusiasm, dynamic and other features as of a new faith. Since the rise of Islam with its far-reaching influence on the spread of the Gospel, there has been no movement so significant as the spread of Communism, and its threat is the most portentous and formidable that the Church has yet had to encounter. The writings of Marx and Lenin now compete with the Bible for the distinction of being the world's best seller. In such a setting it is costly indeed to be a Christian, and it is being shown again that a religion which costs little or nothing is ultimately worth just that. In Dr. John Kelman's words "nothing in this world is so salutory, even so holy, as to face the facts of the case".

There is much study going on as to the appropriate missionary stategy and policy for such a time as this. It is recognised and welcomed that, if a new age of missionary expansion is before us, it will be an age of new pioneering, in relationships between older and younger Churches very different from those which necessarily obtained until the recent past. The day of mission over against Church, with separate centres of authority, is past. The very purpose of separate mission was to work for the day when there would be a Church in these areas to undertake the evangelizing of the people. That time has come, and the missionary contribution of the older Churches which is still needed will be fulfilled in a relationship of close integration and partnership with the younger Churches. It is a situation which has its own adventure and romance but, human nature being what it is, its own diffculties and tensions too.

The only aspect of this complex problem to which a little further thought may be given here is the reunion of the divided Churches, since the unhappy results of disunity are nowhere more evident than in the mission fields. If it be true that only one third of the Church's membership has any interest in the missionary growth of the Church, the proportion concerned about reunion and the ecumenical movement is much smaller; and the kindest excuse for this sad fact that can be offered is that the reunion movement is much younger than the missionary movement.

There is indeed a unity in Christ which all true Christian people already enjoy, an experienced fact for which they do not need to argue and strive. It springs from the very faith of the Gospel. But the surer our possession of that unity is, the deeper our concern must be for the divisions and rivalries which do so greatly hinder the good cause and which have proved such a serious obstacle in the mission areas. The truth as it is in Christ is not to be identified with any one of the Churches, and least of all with any particular structure of the visible Church. Very simple indeed is the Roman view on this subject; but, as it involves mere submission and absorption, it is wholly unacceptable, and is indeed a less than adult solution of the problem. All who are outside Rome have to be on their guard lest they too tend to adopt a view which in spirit is too near the Roman view. There is in several quarters a great deal of laboured effort to prove that a particular conception of Church and Ministry is right, whereas others are not quite right. Some real hope for reunion will arise the more deeply and affectionately we understand that we belong to one another, whatever position we occupy. What is so sad and salutory to remember is that, amid all the fierce controversies in Church relationships in the past and in the more restrained battles of the present, the majority of the people do not go to Church and are not on personal terms with the Gospel.

Do denominational differences seriously cloud the Gospel and mislead men? The extent to which this happens can be exaggerated, and the deterrent force of this situation is probably not nearly so great as the other hindrances already discussed. But this does not absolve the Church of our time from a twofold responsibility—to understand honestly and generously the historic reasons for the divisions, and to confess penitently that we must not perpetuate them. The supreme dynamic behind the reunion movement should be concern for more and better evangelism throughout the whole world scene. It is encouraging that the signs point to an earlier solution of the problem in the younger Churches than in the older, with an ultimate overflow of insight, blessing and stimulus to the mother Churches. Meanwhile, nothing can deny the fact that in the non-Christian lands there has been needless dissension, sectarianism, overlapping and waste, and that this has created an impression that the various Churches and societies were more concerned to propagate their separate selves than to spread the Christian faith. Doubtless again all this aspect of it can be exaggerated, but it has produced a legacy of scorn, resentment and unbelief among the very people that the Churches were there to win. It would be better by far to overestimate the extent to which disunity is a powerful obstacle to world evangelization than to play it and pare it down. To put up all the arguments about the dangers of uniformity and of a monolithic structure—and there is important substance in these objections—can never absolve us from the task of striving for reunion. The advance of the Gospel—nothing less than that —is seriously retarded when people console themselves with the reflection that these divisions do not very much matter or that we should hold on to them because they have existed so long.

The prayer of Jesus Christ—"that they all may be one; as thou, Father, art in me, and I in thee; that they also may be one in us; that the world may believe that thou hast sent me. And the glory which thou gavest me I have given them; that they may be one, even as we are one; I in them and thou in me, that they may be made perfect in one; and that the world may know that thou hast sent me, and hast loved them as thou hast loved me" (John 17, 21–23)—has always been subject to two contrasted forms of extreme interpretation. On one view this has nothing to do with the question of reunion; on the other view that is its chief intention.

At this point in the prayer, Jesus Christ has in mind the Church of the future, those who are to be converted in all ages by the Gospel committed to His apostles and their successors. "Belief cometh by hearing, and hearing by the word of Christ" (Romans 10, 17). All true believers have to be one in Christ, with a depth of unity comparable to the unity of the Father and the Son—"as we are" (John 17, 11). That this is the primary meaning of the prayer cannot be doubted. Such a unity between believers and their Lord will have such effects on their outward life that the world will be impressed and encouraged to believe. The Church remains outwardly divided just because of the want of that fellowship of love. Mature, full-grown Christians will be able to effect visible reunion too. That also is an expression of being "perfected in one". It is quite certain that Jesus Christ intended and founded His Church and that He intended a ministry for His Church, but it is hard to believe that, looking forward, He could have been satisfied with the present divided state of the Church. The unbelieving world is not able to see the invisible unity of the Church, but its visible disunity; and, for this cause among others, they do not believe. In the New Testament the Church is portrayed under three metaphors —as the Body, the Building and the Bride of Christ—and all three point to organic union. Outward separation is not and will not be a great calamity, if it means a rich, wide diversity of expression and method; but that is very different from the kind of division now existing.

The movement of the Churches towards each other in modern times has taken two forms. First, and naturally, there has been a drawing together of Churches akin in confession and polity, and so we have heard much of world Anglicanism, world Presbyterianism, world Congregationalism. Second, there has been an approach to the conception of united Churches from all these backgrounds on a regional or national basis. It is no disparagement to the former to suggest that the latter is more important and promising. The issue cannot and ought not to be separated from the total character of the world scene in our time, for the divided state of the non-Roman Christian world is quietly but ominously giving other forces their big chance. All the appearances are that Communism, having looted from "an unguarded Christian armoury" the powerful weapons of faith and hope, envisages and is preparing for worldwide expansion. The Roman Catholic Church, having experienced in the last generation great setbacks and notable gains, and pursuing its own masterly, united strategy, is probably the second most influential power in the world scene. The prospects for the Reformed faith are very different from half a century or a century ago. Among scholars there has been an immensely quickened interest in the Reformers—but this has not percolated far down. For the very sake of the Reformed faith and in loyalty to the Reformers who had a marked repugnance to schism, the Churches must not slacken the efforts for a visible oneness before men.

It has been a weakness of the ecumenical movement that so far, and perhaps inevitably, its work has been sustained by the theologian, the scholar, and the ordained man with a consequent remoteness from the rank and file of the Churches, the vast majority of whom are uninterested and unmoved. Difficult as it may be, this has to be changed. Just because questions of order and ministry arise so much in all Church relationships, the push will have to come from the laity, and apart from that push it is not easy to contemplate advance. There are two possible eventualities which would, each in its own very different way, make all the difference in this field. The one is a deep, widespread reawakening of true Christianity; the other is a vast, international catastrophe. It is not for us to predict confidently the former, but it is for us to work and pray that the latter may not come and to hope that it may not be true again that the people of God learn too late. In this field, as in others, is sufficient Christian obedience hardly to be expected, except at the spur of gigantic disaster? Can we prevent that by building up a large constituency of Church members who passionately and intelligently hold the conviction so dear to two such different men as John Calvin and Richard Baxter. In a letter of 1552 to Archbishop Cranmer, who died at the stake for the Reformed faith, John Calvin wrote "Among the greatest evils of our time must be counted the fact that the Churches are so disunited. So far as I am concerned, if I can do anything to help, I shall not hesitate to cross ten oceans to serve this cause". To which two sentences from Richard Baxter's autobiography may be added. "I am deeplier afflicted for the disagreements of Christians than I was when I was a younger Christian. Except the case of the infidel world, nothing is so sad and grievous to my thoughts as the case of the divided Churches".

6

Attention must now be given to the theological factor in evangelism. There are deeply-committed and far-seeing servants of the Church who have reached the conclusion that this may well be the leading hindrance to the spread of the Gospel. The question to be faced here is the relation of sound theology and evangelical dynamic. Too often dogmatics and preaching, intended by God to be joined together, have fallen asunder. The all-important enterprize of evangelism would move forward and achieve enduring results, if it was normal for those who are well educated theologically to have the daring, directness and passion of the popular evangelist, and if the popular evangelist had the thorough, theological accuracy and depth which would extend his appeal to many whom it cannot reach at present, which would prevent him from saying things upon occasion which are just not true and which would guarantee more lasting results and less reaction and disillusionment. This happy, effective combination of good theology and good evangelism is too rare.

The word "evangelism" must not be monopolized by those whose fervour is sometimes sensational and bigoted, whose general outlook is narrow and censorious, whose witness is often deeply tainted, though unconsciously, with egoism and self-righteousness. In the true sense of the term they are not evangelical, for they are not declaring the whole counsel of God, the good news of the Gospel in all its power and range, its seriousness and tenderness. True evangelism ought to have no connection with obscurantism in any field or with any of the ugly forms of arrogant dogmatism. There is no good

71

reason why a modern, well-educated and intellectually honest sinner cannot come to personal terms with God in Christ—and many do—provided only that that kind of man does not yield to the wholly unreasonable fallacy, which reason itself should indicate to him to be unreasonable, of trying to settle every issue intellectually before he believes. True faith is the response of the whole being, with the consent of all the faculties, to the supreme reality with which we are confronted; God in Jesus Christ.

The three basic presuppositions of evangelism are all specifically theological. First, there is Christ's view of the world as a lost world, needing to be redeemed and saved. The world has been fully and finally redeemed in Him, and is being saved as it accepts its redemption and all that its redemption implies. From this it follows that the needs of mankind cannot be sufficiently met by culture, education, social activity, pleasure, new standards of living, a changed economic system, or improved international relationships. From the bankruptcy and hopelessness of men's unaided efforts, they have to be brought out of the state of awayness from God to the trust and obedience of God.

Secondly, there is the belief in the power of the supernatural. The Biblical view of the new life is that it is a gift from above, something of which the world as such knows nothing, because it is essentially made possible by the power of God. True evangelism is the manifestation and vindication of this supernatural life, and perhaps the greatest lack in contemporary Church life, especially in the Western world, and America, is the sense of the supernatural. This sense is inseparable from the Christian affirmation that there has been an invasion of earth from heaven, a vertical cleavage of all time and history when the Son of God took upon Himself the form of sinful flesh and was made in the likeness of men.

Thirdly, there follows the conviction that God in Christ is continually challenging all men to decision. Man can and must give a verdict, and indeed is always doing so. There are two words of Jesus Christ which appear contradictory, but in the setting in which they are they are both true. "He that is not with Me is against Me" (Matt. 12, 30)—by that word and its most exacting standard we have to judge ourselves. "He that is not against us is for us" (Luke 9, 50)—by that word and its less exacting standard we may venture to judge others. In either case, neutrality is ruled out; in the inward places of life, it does not exist, whatever the outward appearances are.

The full Gospel which evangelism demands is one that is sustained by certain, grand affirmations for which it has to be claimed that in substance they are either absolutely true or absolutely false, with no middle way, for all time and for all people. Either there is a God, One Personal God of Holy Love, Creator of all, or there is not. Either that God has the nature and character revealed in Jesus Christ, knowing and caring for us one by one, loving us as if there were none else to love, or He has not. Either that God chose to reveal Himself fully in Jesus Christ, fulfilling a drama of perfect love and sacrifice in definite, recognised stages from Bethlehem to the Ascension, each stage having a divine necessity and inevitability about it, or that never happened at all. Either the purpose of all creation is "the appearing of the sons of God" (Romans 8, 23) or it is not. Either this life is the God-appointed scene of introduction to and preparation for personal immortality, or it is not.

All this has an intolerant sound—intolerant indeed as the Bible is intolerant. "I am the Lord and there is none else" (Isaiah 45, 5). "There is no other name under heaven given among men whereby we must be saved" (Acts 4, 12). Toleration is a virtue in reference to the method and spirit in which such a Gospel is proclaimed and advanced. Patience, respect, kindness and humility are utterly essential in the manner in which truth is presented, and it has to be confessed that many exponents of Christianity have grievously failed here. At this point the relation of Christianity to the other world religions arises, as well as its confrontation of all forms of unbelief and materialism. All down the Christian centuries there has been a battle between syncretism, a general amalgam of what seemed best in many creeds, and the unique, special, absolute revelation claimed by Christianity. It is in the very substance of the Christian assertions that the intolerance lies. Vital distinctions must not be lost in a cloud of easy and pleasant generalities collected from many sources. There can be no downgrading of the faith once for all delivered to the saints. This is far removed from the rigidity which is associated with stagnation or death.

All revolt against dogma is ultimately baseless and dangerous. In a recent book, describing submarine warfare, under the unexepected title "The Good Shepherd", the main character says that many vessels were "seaworthy but not battleworthy". It is like that with many Christians, and with preachers too among them. They can keep going on some sort of voyage, but cannot stand up when the fight is on. To be battleworthy for evangelism we need this vital combination of sound theology and evangelical fervour. The confusions in theology have usually been in the form of affirmations "that do not affirm" or of needlessly sharp and misleading antitheses. The substance of theology consists in things that cannot be revised, and the sure grasp of these things engenders evangelical enthusiasm. We have to meet the unbeliever or secularist on his own ground, with friendly interest and patience, willing to learn what he often may have to teach us; but no one of that kind has ever been assisted to faith by paring-down or soft-pedalling the Gospel.

To secure this effective alliance between learning and evangelism has always been a most difficult problem. Theology, divorced from passionate evangelism, as a life and death concern for people, tends to settle into the moulds of arid intellectualism, with reason exercising its devastating dictatorship over all the other elements, insights and faculties of life. Much evangelism, on the other hand, tends to select one element or insight or faculty, a fragment of the whole, and present it as if it were everything, finishing with a kind of "sanctified idolatry" of it. Christianity has always found some of its worst foes within its own household. The warm heart should not be a rival to the clear head, any more than the clear head is a substitute for the warm heart. The Christian will never want a world which has no mysteries, for mysteries are God's glory. A world without mysteries is the bare, ugly dream and desire of ultra-rationalists. As against that, the Christian adoringly accepts the mysteries and yet proclaims that there is "an open secret" in Christ which makes all the difference here and hereafter. The truly theological factor in evangelism keeps all extravagances and irreverences in check, for it takes its stand on the whole organism of Christian truth contained in the Scriptures.

It is the identical function of theology and evangelism to keep men from evading the miraculous fact of Christ and the tremendous challenge of His Person. Every suitable and worthy effort has to be made to transcend the unfortunate contrast which has so frequently arisen between the two, with the result that zeal is unanchored by theological grasp in some quarters, whereas in others intellectualism is such hard soil that no harvest is gathered. It is not to be suggested, however, that all whom the Church seek to win have to be made wise beforehand on all the complex ramifications of theological statement, before they can have any experience of faith. Hungry men do not need to know all the details of the balanced composition of food and of its action on the body before they are persuaded to eat. The disciples rose up and followed before they formulated a creed. "The sincere milk of the Word" comes before "the strong meat".

Evangelism is the best way to set and keep theology on fire, and true theology is the best way to keep the fire of evangelism from undisciplined and harmful forms of emotionalism. T. S. Eliot has reminded us that all the destructive and demonic movements of our time have fire in them—and drive—

> "The only hope or else despair
> Lies in the choice of pyre or pyre,

> To be redeemed from fire by fire;
> We only live, only suspire,
> Consumed by either fire or fire."

Dr. John Mackay's comment on these lines is, "In its full Christian setting and significance this means that fire engendered by man's consuming passion for self-centred satisfaction at all the diverse human levels, from the lower to the higher, or the fire engendered by the Holy Spirit which purifies and enflames man's heart to seek God's Kingdom and righteousness" is man's final choice.

A Church must have certain marks if it is faithfully to represent the full Gospel to our times and be the instrument in the hand of God for such a reawakening and extension of Christianity in the second half of the twentieth century as the world has not yet seen. It has to be a Church wholly committed to the positive doctrine of the authority of Scripture, a Church with a truly dogmatic theology based on a deep understanding of Scripture, a Church stripped of fear of what emerges in the fields of science and psychology, though as deeply concerned as others about possible applications of new knowledge, a Church friendly to all forms of human study and willing to welcome truth from whatever quarter it comes, a Church with an unwearying evangelical earnestness, seeking for true conversions and disappointed and frustrated if they are not forthcoming, a Church bent on an endless crusade to keep alive and alert the social conscience, so that the Kingdom may come.

CHAPTER THREE

The Central Theological Dilemma

IN EVERY generation there have been people who sincerely believed and vigorously advocated that being a Christian is essentially a private, personal relationship of faith in and surrender to Jesus Christ, without radical implications for the life of the community in all its aspects. On the other hand, there have always been people for whom Christianity was understood just in terms of social betterment, salvation being interpreted in the sense of the advance of better living conditions, the general extension of humanitarianism, and freedom from the many-sided injustice of earthly life. The antithesis which is implied in these sentences should not be pressed to the extreme, but the two points of view are sufficiently distinct and antagonistic to be the starting-point of our further discussion.

If these two positions should be regarded as mutually exclusive, they would then both be gravely out of touch with the Bible, with the teaching of the Old Testament prophets (Jer. 22, 13–16) and our Lord's teaching on the Kingdom. It would be a dangerous form of disloyalty to Jesus Christ, if we found ourselves pressed to take one or other of these attitudes. That has to be remembered especially by those who are over-confident that they are exceptionally loyal to Him when they accept and welcome the one standpoint at the cost of the total rejection of the other. There is indeed no such person as a completely God-centred person, least of all when that very term is interpreted either in a sharply individualist sense or in a blurred social sense. The things of the soul and the things of the world cannot be so isolated from each other as that. There are many good people who would be shocked equally by the outright denial of Christianity, in the sense that the unbeliever and materialist tries to deny it, and by the thorough application of Christianity in the spheres of industry, finance, politics and race.

It has to be admitted that some Christians are too other-worldly, "so heavenly-minded as to be of no earthly use". They tend to denounce sadly or vociferously the too worldly Christians with their Utopias and their blue-prints for realising them. The dilemma lies just here. Has the Church a word of challenge for the *this world* situation? Can it be declared unequivocally in Christ's name that He has the word of power to banish fear and injustice and to bring peace and prosperity to all? Is it all so simple as that? What is a Christian world in terms of life upon this planet? Christianity, although the second youngest of the world's religions, has already become more truly and evidently a world-religion than any of the others. The evidence for that is manifest and impressive. Does that imply the ultimate total sovereignty of Jesus Christ?

The present perilous state of the world has inevitably accentuated the agelong tension between the world-denying and the world-transforming emphases of the Christian religion. These emphases are indeed both there. That is the central theological dilemma. The whole urgent, if elusive, subject of the prospects for Christianity as a world-religion is bound up in the dilemma, and as a result so are very big questions of evangelism and missionary strategy.

Will Christianity survive as a world-religion? Is it intended to be this? What are the implications in our daily use of the Lord's Prayer, "Thy Kingdom come, Thy will be done on earth as it is in heaven"? Is the Cross for our example and irritation as well as for our redemption and deliverance? How comprehensive is the Gospel? Is Jesus Christ to be Lord in some fuller sense than in the sovereign control he exercises over the soul, mind and body of the converted and consecrated individual? Has He gathered up into His full Gospel the promise and vision of the closing verses of Psalm 72, and indeed of the whole Psalm and of many parallel passages that resound in the Old Testament? If so, has the Church signally failed to teach this, and allowed the great tides of life to flow outside it and past it? And, if that be so, can we hope that history will not prove itself relentlessly merciless to such a failure?

The Christian religion is likely to be a subject of controversy and even opposition to the end of time. Our Lord Himself did ask the question "When the Son of Man cometh, shall He find faith on the earth?" (Luke 18, 8). The warning which is in these words must never be explained away, but the passage does not mean, as has been often suggested, that it is certain that the human situation must deteriorate seriously before He comes again.

It is highly improbable that men will succeed in controlling the human situation without periodic world-wide catastrophes, unless life is more consciously related to the God and Father of our Lord Jesus Christ than it has ever yet been. History has hitherto been strewn with the wreckage of civilizations that were once strong and secure; but these calamities were in some measure within control, whereas in the modern world they look like getting beyond control. Responsible leaders feel obliged to speak of the end of all civilization as one of the ominous possibilities before mankind. Man by his own unaided efforts cannot come within sight of putting things right and keeping them right. A modern nativity play, "Miracle of Midnight", speaks of the world "stumbling obliviously to its own oblivion" in "luxurious ruin". Christians can be in no doubt of the ultimate cause of such a dark eventuality; but Christians have most reason of all to hold that, while it may be so and even in certain conditions must be so, it need not be so. They hold it certain that the world as such does not know or possess the new life of God's Kingdom. This does not imply that all human effort in the search for knowledge and in the practical applications of knowledge is of the devil, for God is truly at work in at least a large part of what man strives for and achieves. The Kingdom, however, is supernatural in character, breaking through into the natural order. It is the gift of God, manifests itself in ways of life which are consciously related to God, nourished by prayer, worship, service, and obedience to a Divine Law which is true and unchangeable. In all this there is much that is not only mystifying to the modern mind but most unpalatable to the modern taste.

2

In Church life, the period since the end of the second World War has been marked by a thorough discussion of the essential obligation and the varied techniques of evangelism. It is highly probable that there has never been so much questing and experiment in this field. Not since the days of the Apostles has the responsibility for evangelism been laid so squarely and urgently upon the membership of the Church as a whole, but there is widespread hesitation and bewilderment in beginning the effort to fulfil that responsibility.

It is no part of this argument to belittle the main activities being carried on by the modern Church, nor is it questioned that the best missionary to a congregation is normally its own minister. There is no evangelism worthy of the name which does not stress the central need for personal surrender and consecration, daring to proclaim that the plight of all men is hopeless apart from Christ, and resting content with nothing less than the building up of converts in their faith and life by means of the fellowship and service of the

80

Church. Revivals which group people outside the Church in sects have gone far astray. Even the greatest revivals lose their impetus all too soon. Good results from them are undeniable, often over a long period. But the evidence of relapse is serious and disturbing. This may be accounted for in various ways—an ineffective follow-up, the inevitable break-up of an effervescent, emotional experience, the reawakening of the natural resistance to the Gospel, the blight of lethargy, or the malady of not really wanting the new life which has been described as the worst of all maladies. In addition to all this, there is the deep failure of the revival movement to integrate itself sufficiently with all aspects of life. A very important subject for careful study would be the relationship or want of relationship between the Wesleyan revival and the Industrial Revolution. How closely did they impinge upon each other? Did they largely by-pass each other? There is also the undoubted fact that some zealous evangelicals in Victorian and modern times have been most influential upholders of the status quo in society. This did not necessarily mean that they were consciously hypocritical, but that they erroneously believed that religion belonged to one compartment and politics to another compartment of life, and that all questions of the better and juster ordering of society had to be kept outside a religious meeting. The logic of this is that religion will be excluded from politics altogether.

The gap has now become alarmingly wide. As science has advanced and as the industrial age has been built up, it seems to be increasingly obvious that all the activity of ordinary Church life and of special missions, while seldom without its beneficial results, is not able to stir the community to any notable degree, or to establish itself as utterly relevant to the needs and strivings of community life. This is not to be accounted for entirely by the carelessness and peversity of human beings in all matters relating to God and the soul. No one has ever proceeded far in evangelism without encountering that stubborn barrier. Even if the major social, economic and political problems were solved, the

Church's main task in dealing with this barrier would remain, for original sin and its consequences will not be superseded.

But the dilemma just is that there is another factor. Is there not some acute division of view within the Church itself on some vital part of Christian doctrine? If so, that may be producing a paralysing hesitation as to the relevance of the Gospel in relation to the whole life of man in history. There is little doubt that in the past great social reforms were instigated by evangelical revival and led forward by men and women who drew their dynamic from their personal Christian experience. Sometimes unfortunately the most illustrious Christian social reformers such as Howard, Shaftesbury and Wilberforce, received small support from the Church as a whole and even met adamant opposition from it at times. There has been, however, a serious change for at least the last half century. The main passion for social improvement has flowed through other channels, either openly secularist or only tenuously connected with Christ. In our time much of the most active enterprize of this kind is in the hands of those who owe no open allegiance to Him at all. These have their big opportunity because it is a simple fact that great masses of the human race are still at the low stage of development at which they are prepared to give away almost every kind of freedom for the sake of the economic uplift which is being held out to them.

It is most likely that the area of agreement in the field of doctrine is much larger in our time, as between the various Churches than it was not so long ago. This rests solidly on a deeper and wider agreement between the Churches on the main content of the Biblical message. It is a happy experience that, when representatives of different Churches which are deeply divided on such issues as the doctrines of the Church, the Ministry and the Sacraments meet together, they are agreeably surprised to find how much else they hold in common. Even here there is room for caution, because it is still dangerously easy to overestimate the amount of doctrinal agreement. There are indeed profound divergences on such subjects as the authority and inspiration of the Bible, the inner meaning of the Atonement, the Second Coming of our Lord, and the final destiny of sinful man; but these tensions cut across all the other denominational boundaries.

What is quite certain is that the area of disagreement has widened in at least one of the cardinal doctrines—the doctrine of the Kingdom of God. In no field of theology is there more need for sustained Bible study. Without clarification of this doctrine, there must be great uncertainty in the grasp and the proclamation of the doctrines of redemption and judgment. There is a close connection also between this uncertainty about the Kingdom and the lethargic pace at which the reunion movement proceeds, for unless we see how "our unhappy divisions" stultify all efforts to make the life of the Kingdom evident upon this earth, we will not be touched with any quickening enthusiasm for it.

Hence the central dilemma lies in the realm where doctrine has especially to translate itself into action. The slogan "Christ or Chaos", which has been used in many a campaign, is misleading when it is superficially conceived, and has often raised false hopes; and yet there is an important, ultimate sense in which it is utterly true. To deny or overlook this is to commit ourselves to a wholly otherworldly view, of which the following is perhaps an extreme statement, and to which large numbers of Christians are being driven by the state of the world today. In his book "Christianity and Race" Philip Mason quotes two ministers of the Dutch Reformed Church thus—"I think I am right in saying that neither Christ nor the Apostles ever went beyond the preaching of the Gospel of salvation and warning against wrong attitudes of mind. I do not think that they ever concerned themselves with the politics of the day". "Christ did not want to be the great reformer, even though He was conscious of the fact that there was great need for reformation. He did not come to this world to relieve tensions or to reform the world, but to save sinners from sin. He did proclaim a Kingdom but it was the Kingdom of God and not the kingdom of this world".

Have not these speakers fallen into the peril of the false antithesis? Jesus Christ is the Saviour of the individual soul and of society. His followers need to think much of the state of their souls and of the state of the world. In His parables of the rich man and Lazarus (Luke 16, 19–31) and of the Last Judgment (Matthew 25, 31–46), the main lesson is in the region of man's inhumanity to man. Christ takes in all the issues of life, personal and public. When we are saved, it is always with a new concern of love for all that affects our neighbour, for such love is His new commandment. The teaching of Christ is certainly timeless, but it is also timely and contemporary. He makes us alert to the practical realities of the situation everywhere. There is a true sense in which it is for the Church to feed and not to stifle moral indignation with all forms of social wrong wherever they appear. If not, multitudes will look in another direction, as indeed they are doing.

An example of the theological confusion with which we are now dealing may be given. A few years ago, in a long, animated debate in the General Assembly of the Church of Scotland on Communism in the modern world, the following resolution was unanimously carried. "The General Assembly urge upon all Ministers the task of interpreting these grave events in the light of the fundamental truth of the Bible, with its unbroken unity of personal and social implication and obligation, and proclaiming anew their faith that it is the Will of God to bring in a Kingdom in which the whole structure of community life is brought into the allegiance of Christ". The reactions to this were significant. Some were overjoyed to find the Church making so unequivocal a declaration. Others said that, if the Church really believed this, a big obstacle to effective evangelism was removed. In other quarters it was pronounced to be substantially at variance with the New Testament revelation. Some went so far as to say that such Utopian dreams were not only out of touch with common sense but obscured the fact that the children of God live and will always live in a world which is the devil's.

In these contrasted attitudes lies the central dilemma of evangelism. What does the Church really believe on this vital issue? Is the Church continually speaking with two voices on the doctrine of the Kingdom? It is not indeed given to us to know how long the drama of human life is to be continued upon this earth. But, if it should be the Will of God that history be prolonged for aeons to come, what has the Church to say concerning the impact of Christianity upon all our social structures? If in point of fact Christianity is still in its infancy as a world religion, if the time before it should be immensely long compared with the short period it has already existed, what do we believe about the range and the depth of its transforming influence upon all life? If in less than two thousand years it has achieved so much as it has certainly done, what are the ultimate prospects, if there may be millions of years of history for mankind before us? If mankind is to have a far future, is it to be a Christian future? All other tensions in evangelism are marginal compared with this one.

In an age of great prosperity and optimism, Tennyson could say,

> "We are far from the noon of man,
> There is time for the race to grow."

If that is conceivably true, despite the torments and alarms of the present century, despite even the possibility of an era of vast ruin, under what supreme influence is that upward process to be moulded and matured? The main part of the attack of the Gospel is and always will be directed to those who are convinced that the spiritual is false, untrue, unreal or irrelevant—"the science-worshipping agnostics" and others who know less of that attitude but to whom something of that general view has percolated down. There is no reason to suppose that assured social security and prosperity would do away with basic unbelief, for these might well strengthen it in some quarters. Also, as Brunner would put it, the social order is but the frame into which the real life is poured. Nevertheless, when we do succeed in piercing the barrier of unbelief, we are still faced with the large problem of the new order.

3

There is agreement in most Christian circles that we are bound by the Scriptures to believe that God has a plan for this world. What is it, and how is it to be realized? Is Christ the Saviour not only of individuals *out of* the sinful world, but also of the world itself (John 4, 42; 17, 8–9; 1 John 4, 14), and even of all God's creation (Romans 8, 22–28). If the choice really lay between converting individuals and building a Christian society, the former would have to come first, in all loyalty to the New Testament emphasis and method. But no such choice is before us. A sane and forthright evangelism covers both personal commitment and sacrificial dedication to the tasks of the Kingdom which are implied in the commitment.

In the modern human situation, there are several alarming gulfs. First there is the obvious one between man's intellectual achievement and his character, ever reminding us that cleverness is no substitute for goodness. Again, on the whole it seems to be fair to say that man's aspirations for better living conditions are greater than his aspirations for his own conversion. In our "entertainment-drugged" society, no assumption is more easy than that religion is a soft, optional extra. This produces the further gap between inward conviction and a too blind confidence in outward action. God's plan for His world is based on right belief, issuing in right action in every sphere. All false views of man rest in the last resort on false views of God. Man cannot truly believe in himself or grasp the meaning and purpose of his life unless he first believes in God. If these dangerous chasms can be bridged by Christ, the consequences in all life will be manifest and widespread. Christianity has rightly been held to combine a this-worldly mission with an other-worldly hope. The central dilemma of evangelism is our uncertainty as to the objectives of the this-worldly mission, beyond personal conversion and a share in corporate worship.

The message of the Kingdom has never been held in the form of a perfected society on earth. We have no reason to suppose that sin and death, the two main enemies of a perfected society, are ever to be completely conquered here. Our final satisfaction could never lie in a perfect earthly society, with nothing at all to strive for any more. Every life brings its own evil into the world, as well as its own good. That will always be so, unless we could conceive some radical change in the very constitution of human nature, by which it would be set free completely from the grip of original sin. But that belongs to the life of heaven, after we have stepped outside the limitations of the body and of time itself. Even if the Church in some real sense were to win the allegiance of everybody, this would still be true. The Church in these circumstances would not be the equivalent of the Kingdom of God, but only a promise of and an approximation to the heavenly commonwealth. But do we believe as much as that to be implied in the New Testament Gospel? Nothing but harm is done by the confusion of the essential and the derivative, but the derivative may well have far greater significance and importance than is often assigned to it in theological thought, and so it may now deserve more careful and respectful attention.

Many Christian writers in our day have in effect said that the sole purpose of preaching the Gospel is the gathering together of the community which waits for the Lord's return. Others have said that the goal of all Christian witness is the Kingdom of God. What precisely is involved? Are these two groups saying virtually the same thing? This causes deep uneasiness, discomfort and frustration in the inward thoughts of many a preacher, and there is a restless groping for some sure word along the line of "Christian action", some compelling sense of the relevance of the full Gospel to the whole future of mankind.

The dilemma may be further stated in these terms. In modern mass society, or for that matter in any kind of society, has the Church any further task than to win the allegiance of individuals to Christ by their repentance and faith, to build them up in the worshipping fellowship of the Church, and to look for the Parousia as the climax and consummation of the whole human drama? All would surely agree that all this is centrally important. But is there nothing more in Christianity? The Church much needs to be more agreed and definite on this issue.

When the World Council of Churches met at Evanston in 1955, its theme was "Christ the Hope of the World", and the burden of its message was that "there is salvation in Christ for the whole life of man, that the Gospel is the only means of deliverance both for the Church and the world". All the other themes that were considered were regarded as subsidiary to this. What does this in fact imply for the Church? There was wide divergence revealed on this issue at the World Council, and a resultant feeling of confusion and indecision.

Professor Arnold Toynbee in a book "Civilization on Trial" maintains that there are three conditions necessary for world survival—to establish a constitutional, co-operative system of world government, to find an economic synthesis by working compromises between free enterprise and socialism and to set the whole secular superstructure of things upon a religious foundation. He leaves the reader in no doubt that he estimates the third requirement as the all-important one. He also indicates fairly clearly that he regards the only really sound foundation as a Christian one, although in a later book "The Religion of an Historian" he argues that the religion of the future must be an amalgam of the best elements of all religions—which is a conception alien to the Bible and contrary to the genius of Christianity which has historically claimed to be the final and absolute religion for men in virtue of its distinctive declarations on God, man and destiny.

In the earlier book, Professor Toynbee examines three views of the meaning and purpose of human life. First, there is a purely this-world view which asserts that the whole of existence is contained in space and time and within earthly history. Second, there is the purely other-world view which asserts that the complete meaning of existence is outside earthly history in the unseen and eternal world. Third, there is the view that this world is intended to be a province of the Kingdom of God. He rejects the first two views in favour of the third. So we are left asking again—"how much is meant by saying that this world is intended to be a province of the Kingdom of God?"

So the perplexity grows. In one of our cities a few years ago a "teaching mission" was undertaken by the Churches, with a carefully-prepared syllabus. It was a surprise to many that the theme of the Kingdom of God was not included, and it was revealed that it had not been found possible to reach agreement on what should be said to the people on that doctrine. When the Church of Scotland a quarter of a century ago accepted "a Short Statement of the Christian Faith", compiled by eminent theologians, there was no section at all on the Kingdom. During the years of war the students of a theological college gathered to hear an address on "The Concept of Christian Civilization". It was just at a time when leading statesmen were continually declaring that the war was being fought to save Christian civilization. The substance of the argument was that the phrase is a misnomer, that there never has been and never will be "a Christian civilization" and that it was wrong to speak of defending it. Further that the life of this world might and probably would be improved by political and social efforts, but that it was not an essential part of historic Christianity to work for a society which, because it is moulded more and more to the mind and spirit of Christ, might worthily be called a Christian society. It seemed to be taken for granted that we could never hope to convert enough Christians to make such a society conceivable. One of the speakers in the discussion singled out as a serious departure from the Church's true function the setting up of committees dealing with "Church and Nation", and he vigorously advanced the view that the Church stood over against the nation, seeking to gather out of the nation such as were being saved. This speaker also indulged in much criticism of most of the hymns of the Kingdom, and it was known that he was fully in agreement with a group of students in the college who, whenever a hymn of the Kingdom suggesting a transformed world was given out at College prayers, stood silent, with a look of grim, eschatological defiance upon their faces.

At the close of this lecture, the presiding professor recognised its ability but added that it was a very cold douche for those beginning their ministry. Another most learned and saintly Churchman, as he left, groaned out "Deplorable pessimism". Was he not really nearer to the full content of the New Testament revelation? On the view advanced in the lecture, there is no ultimate reason why the Church should be concerned about the state of the world. Many, however, feel today that one of the big weaknesses of the situation is that the Church is too disintegrated from the world's life, and sheltering behind a false, non-Biblical distinction between the sacred and the secular. The first World Council of Churches at Amsterdam, when it dealt with this issue, contented itself with listing the blemishes and errors of laissez-faire capitalism and materialistic communism, and said that an alternative, constructive solution had to be found. What, then, is the Church's part in that solution? Where does the Gospel come into it, if at all? That is the central dilemma of modern evangelism.

4

The field in which this debate is proceeding most vigorously is in the theology and eschatology of missions. There are divisions here which run across all the Churches. It is more than a difference of emphasis that emerges here. The main features of one of the two veiwpoints may be summarized thus.

It is admitted that the facts of the expansion of Christianity are in themselves impressive, and not least in the period of modern missions covering almost the last two hundred years. The religion of Jesus Christ has taken root in every soil and won the allegiance of some in every race. But there have also been serious relapses and retreats, and in every century Christianity has been opposed and persecuted. Churches that were once strong have grown feeble, younger Churches have frequently succumbed all too soon to the weaknesses and errors of the older Churches, some Churches have virtually disappeared, and the Christian community is a small minority tending to grow smaller in the areas where population is most rapidly increasing. The phrase which is much used nowadays, "the Church under the Cross", is held to describe what the Church has always been and must necessarily always be. This is interpreted as being fully within the purpose and providence of God.

Such a view as this can quickly develop into escapist pietism and self-stultifying defeatism, unless it be kept in close correspondence with a sure belief in the Second Coming of Christ. So indeed it is in our time which has seen a revival of emphasis on the doctrine of the Second Coming which had fallen into a secondary place. It is not the full teaching of the Bible that the triumph of God will take place at last only in eternity, for it is also promised that there will be a real triumph of God, achieved by the act of God, in time and history. The fulfilment of the stage in God's dealing with the world in which we are now involved is that God will again intervene in glory and that that will be the climax and consummation of history. The Church, the new Israel, is therefore a remnant upon the earth, and as such it is the instrument by which God is preparing the world for and leading up to this final stage, just as the old Israel was His instrument for preparing the world for His intervention in Christ. The "last days", then, mean the whole final stage from the First Advent to the Second Advent of our Lord.

On the basis of all this, the missionary task of the Church is clear—to preach the Gospel to all peoples, not in the hope of converting the whole world to Christ, but as a preparation for His coming in great glory. If we see no evident sign of the conversion of the peoples on a larger scale, we need not be surprised or disappointed. We do see the faithful remnant in every country, getting ready to receive Him when He comes again. The Church has no strength adequate to vast schemes of world conversion, and it is urged that we should be straightforward and realistic about this. The slogan which stirred so many nearly two generations ago, "the evangelization of the world in our generation" was not intended to imply the expectation of a wholesale acceptance of Christ, but to call for such a use of the Church's existing resources as would bring all men within a generation within the hearing of the Gospel, whatever their response might be.

It is an essential part of this view that the hope which arises for mankind out of the advances of scientific knowledge and all the other endeavours of secular progress is of a very different sort from the hope which springs out of Christian faith—and also much more precarious. The world may be regarded as "enemy-occupied territory" and the Church is God's "resistance movement", appointed to operate as such to "the end of history". The only way in which evangelism can be truly expectant is by looking to this end. "The Church in history is the Church of the interim", and the only way for it to be faithful to the message of the Kingdom is to detach itself from all secular hopes, and to persist in doing so, even though it may plan for tens of thousands of years to come.

Those who maintain the other main viewpoint in the theology of missions have grave misgivings about the attitude which has just been described. They feel for one thing that it plays into the hands of the cruder kind of Second Adventists who are very rife in the mission field and who are doing such a big disservice to the Christian cause everywhere. Is the position which has been outlined as truly Biblical as it claims to be? There is involved in it a radical, irreconcileable opposition existing between Christ's society and all other societies, whatever working compromises and amicable adjustments may be necessary. Would not theology of this type accelerate the process which is already well under way in the Church by which the Church gives up one piece of territory after another which it used to occupy, and so becomes increasingly disintegrated from the community-life all around? Is the Church meant by its Divine Founder to be a close, intimate fellowship, in the sense of a society within society, but never hoping for the transformation of all society? Without accepting the view that the Kingdom of God in its completeness can be built here and now, and wholly accepting the view that there must be a signal, final victory of good by the act of God, we may still ask if there is not another strain of thought in the Bible which suggests that the preaching of Christianity will yet yield greater evidence of its truth and power in this world, as the long process moves to its consummation. The Church must not be too easily satisfied with its present status as a minority movement, too speedily reconciled to the view that a large part of the world is permanently lost. It is surely a very open question whether the general sense of Scripture necessarily supports the view that the Church is only here to prepare the world for the consummation.

The conception that it is the *desire* of God to win all men is also in the New Testament (1 Tim. 2, 1–4; Titus 2, 11:

John 5, 23; Phil. 2, 9–10). That the whole earth could become a new Christendom (for the old Christendom has gone), is not necessarily a mistaken or presumptuous hope —but this is not the same as the bringing home of all souls to God at last. Principal David S. Cairns, in a study of the famous missionary hymns ("International Review of Missions", April 1942), argued that it is not to be just a "ding-dong battle" all the way, with the good becoming better and the bad becoming worse, right on to the end. The missionary hymns are almost without exception on the side of a theology of missions which envisages a Christendom built on this earth, for they are full of vision and hope, and contemplate with assurance a conversion of all races and nations. In the light of these hymns, the Advent is not to be understood solely in terms of judgment. Are these hymns so radically wrong that their use should be discarded? Have we not rather to face up more fully and bravely to all that is implied in the belief that God is by nature creative and redeeming Love, that His justice and judgment are not rival principles to His Love, but essential manifestations of it? The God revealed in Christ has a far deeper interest in even the secular civilizations and the human beings who compose them than in passing judgment upon them. When all is said that deserves to be said about the perils of social enthusiasms pointing to various types of Paradise on earth, and the misconception of being more preoccupied with the under-privileged than with the unconverted, it still remains true as Dr. Cairns put it, that "in the Church we have the potentiality at least of effecting the enormous change that is necessary to make a real Christendom out of our very faulty, corrupt simulacrum of it". Professor Oscar Cullmann, in his famous book, "Christ and Time", made a most important contribution to this discussion. He distinguishes very clearly between "decisive battle" and "victory day". In a long campaign the battle which virtually decides the issue is usually distinct from the final battle and makes the issue of the final battle certain. For Christianity the decisive battle with evil was in the death and Resurrection of Jesus Christ. Two thousand years have passed, but the final victory day has not yet come. We may be misreading the times if we are too dogmatically convinced that it is just at hand in our twentieth century. In the long stretch of history, Christianity is still comparatively a newcomer upon the scene. Must we not work for still more impressive evidence here of the victory of the forces of the Gospel, in the belief that that is the Will of God?

5

As the Church pursues its missionary task, it is kept up by that very work to the high levels of vision, prayer, penitence and obedience; and there is no other way in which that can be achieved. The Church learns afresh what the true essence of Christianity is, and there is always an overflow from the missionary outreach which makes the inward spirit of the Church more sharp, vigorous, alert, resourceful and catholic.

In the modern age there has been a fresh, searching scrutiny into the true missionary motive. Such motives as compassion for human beings and still more the prestige of established Churches are secondary. Christian love in the full sense of the term is the supreme motive. So it was in the apostolic age, so it was at the start of the modern missionary movement. Christian love can leave nobody out and can make no exception of nation, race, class or creed. The world is not going to be saved just by a more comprehensive dogmatic system, but Christian love in action will produce a fuller and truer theology. God has joined these two together, and it is not for man to put them asunder. The insights and the compulsions of the actual missionary task,

95

conceived in its full Biblical sense, provide an adequate basis for a deeper and more compelling theology. The doctrine of the Catholic Church, transcending all barriers and boundaries, has little reality except in the missionary situation. A corrective is much needed to all sectional, parochial views of the Church, and it is supplied best by the work of making known the Gospel to all nations. When the emphasis is primarily denominational, the result is a denominational theology too. True theology is attainable only in the context of the universal Church, and it is for the universal Church to lead the way in the living liaison between the this-worldly and the other-worldly elements in the Kingdom.

It is used to be said that Professor Willard Sperry of Yale invariably failed a student who claimed to solve the social and the international problem in the final paragraph of a sermon. There is warning enough in that. The Church has to be unquestioningly loyal to all that the New Testament says about the new life as a supernatural gift from above. "The whole creation is on tiptoe to see the wonderful sight of the sons of God coming into their own" (Romans 8, 19:). Man's sin is indeed "a frightful deadlock", but God has undertaken the solution. In grace He plans the reconciliation of all things in Christ. So we cannot have this new life in any full sense without many social implications. It is personal but not private and selfish. If that is so, then we can proceed with real meaning and not in trite emptiness to say that Christ is the only remedy for the world's discords, that He alone can guarantee right relationships. In the last generation, many preachers have declared from their pulpit such things as "it has to be a Christian world-order or no world-order at all", "God has shown us the way to unity and peace in this world", "there is a Christian solution to every problem", "the world can have peace tomorrow on God's terms". Are these assertions justifiable? To refer again to the slogan "Christ or chaos" which has become discredited in many quarters, must we distinguish sharply between having Christ for Himself (which all would agree is supreme) and Christ for His benefits? Or can we escape from the painful dilemma by saying "Even if it be chaos, nevertheless Christ". In a true context that is undoubtedly right, and few who have ever placed a positive emphasis on the offending slogan would ever deny it. It was, however, another point that they were striving to conserve.

On this whole issue of the influence of Christianity on the community-aspects of life it is scarcely enough to say to individuals, "You go out into society, industry and politics and make your witness there, holding high the flag". We had better remember that some men would make themselves decidedly unpopular and even lose their job, if they carried that advice to its right conclusion. Yet the Church is not meant to be a kind of Noah's ark, a ship in which a favoured or a specially alert few escape from the storms of life and are preserved from ultimate destruction. If so, the Church's task is relatively easy, and we do not need to lament that the great tides of unbelieving life are sweeping past us, or to be concerned and frustrated because of the evident failure to make impact in Christ's name on the whole structure of things. It is indeed vastly important to be able to tell people what they have to believe to be Christian, but they will go on asking what we are to do, in the light of that belief and by its dynamic, to help build a better world here. How frequently we encounter the phrase "the lordship of Christ over the whole life of mankind"; it occurs in the most recent statement of the aim of the Student Christian Movement. Can there be such a lordship while great areas of life deny Him? Is that to be regarded as normal in a fallen world? Is He to be Lord over a ruined world?

The motto of the Jocists and other kindred societies is "to put the whole of Christianity into the whole of life". What exactly does that mean? Is it conceivably possible? The priests who in wartime renounced everything to go out and seek to win the godless workers believed that their mission did not lie in creating individual Christians only but in advancing a Christian community, with a Christian civilization as the great goal. They felt that the workers' world had to be saved as well as the workers. They maintained that the present theological emphasis on eschatology was essential as a corrective. But what may well be needed as a corrective may degenerate into an obsession; and all obsessions are escapist, flights away from the hard facts.

Christianity must not lead a retreat into individualism and quietism, nor concentrate all its emphasis on personal conversion and piety. Some Christian groups are in danger of shifting the emphasis from the objective truths of the Gospel to its pragmatic value for society; but others have succumbed to the opposite danger of failing to recognise the social implications and obligations of the Gospel. "High-minded social ethics and politics" is not religion, but real religion ought to include these and to provide an unfailing spur towards them. Up to the present Christianity has been largely powerless to cope with the problems and tensions of the modern industrial age, and has sought refuge too promptly in the assertion that you can be a good Christian under any social and political system. Is this want of relevance to the problems of the age to be understood as inherent in Christianity itself, or is it a tragic failure? Communism offers itself as the solution of all these problems, but leaves out immense tracts of truth and insight which are vital to Christianity. Has Christianity no alternative word to speak in respect of these very problems for which Communism aggressively claims to be the solution? It is indeed this offer of Communism which is the primary, if not the sole, explanation of its phenomenal advance. It is an error to equate democracy with the Kingdom of God, but not an error to claim that true democracy is the fruit of evangelical Christianity. The roots of freedom and democracy are in God Himself and their decay is sure when they cut themselves off from their source. For a long time now we have heard laments that the Church has lost the working classes, and it has been powerfully argued that it never really had them. How shall we hope to regain them if we cannot say that the conception of a Christian community in all areas of life is an integral part of the Gospel? A Christian civilization on earth must legitimately be regarded as coming within the Kingdom of God. We are paying a heavy price today for the two heresies of nationalized Christianity and individualized Christianity. The Church which will truly serve her Master's purposes is a Church which at one and the same time is separate from the world and yet unceasingly involved in every aspect of the struggle of history, to the end that it be an upward struggle.

Professor Emil Brunner gave an address some years ago on "The Church in the New World Order" which definitely divided the audience. "The interest of the Church in any given social order can only be indirect. Its primary task is not to fight for a social programme, but to preach the Gospel of eternal life. Christians, sensitive to the former aloofness of the Church to social questions, are now going too far the other way, thinking that the Church's supreme business is to change the social order. The Kingdom of God is not a new social order for men to create, but new life that only God can bring about. The more man has this new life, the less he will be like "opium", and the more he will be "motor" for the new order. Christianity, however, is more social than socialism, more communal than any communism".

Most people would accept all this, so far as it goes, but some would find it necessary to set alongside of it what Professor Jessop says in "Social Ethics, Christian and Natural". Probably the emphasis made by Professor Jessop is more necessary than the other. He believes that the Church is spiritually illiterate in a secularized society, and that there is urgent need for the education of Christians both in the faith in general and in the social doctrines in particular. Otherwise he fears that the tendency will grow among Christians of "throwing up our hands and waiting for the dreadful apocalypse". The Church has lost its grip in guiding society. He sees that big social changes have come and will come fast, but he fears that they may be without religious reasons and motives, brought about by jealousy, hate and greed, and so essentially different from those that could be brought about by sympathy and love. The awakened social conscience may be nothing more than the bottom dog struggling to be top dog. The Church, he holds, has to be profoundly and inescapeably concerned with the structure of earthly society and the motivation of social change. Although it is a blunder for the Church to set up its own political bandwaggon, it is heresy to say that the Church has nothing to do with politics. He regards it as disastrous for the cause of Christianity that, not only is there no specifically Christian doctrine of society which the Church teaches its people, but that many in the Church would regard such a thing as a grave distortion of Christianity, even though many theologians in the middle ages and John Calvin at a later date would deny that it is a distortion. Christianity is a deeply social religion, and society too has to be made subject to God's Will. So there must be a will of God for industry and international relationships. This, he holds, is a lost idea. The sovereignty of God is not complete without its recovery. Society has to be so ordered as to serve God's great aim for our full development. It is not for the state to make Christians, but to provide the conditions in which that transforming change can be more possible. So there is an essential relationship between our earthly and our heavenly citizenship. That in itself is a big reason for improving the conditions of this world. "It is a real want in a man", says Amiel in his Journal, "when his mind is always in Church". And Dr. William Temple went so far as to state that "Christianity is the most avowedly materialistic of all religions". Since the Word was made flesh, the universe is sacramental. There is profound and ultimate meaning in the process of human history, and it is the function of Christianity to mould and control the process in His name and by His power.

It has been a great gain to witness in modern theology a

recovery of the sense of a transcendent God. But that should express itself not in an escape from the problems which mean so much to ordinary people on this earth, but in a radical sociology and a programme which is revolutionary by conventional standards. The Church has to be behind demands for social justice and freedom, in God's great name. So Principal John A. Mackay, while careful not to identify Christianity with civilization, goes on to say that "Christianity has to reverse the downward drag of history. The Church is the servant of the Gospel and must proclaim re-creation and redemption to the whole human situation". At certain historic moments in the long struggle between Church and State in Scotland, it was claimed that Jesus Christ had certain inalienable "crown rights" in His Church. We have to extend the claim into every realm, personal and social, scientific and aesthetic, national and international.

Quite apart from questions of method and technique, it seems certain that there are three requisites for evangelism. The first is the drawing of dynamic from past history. As we lift up the veil of history, we can discern a Supreme Providence ruling all other wills, without ever faltering or failing. The second is the sure vindication that comes from experience. Our own love for Christ impels us to share that love. The measure in which we prize our faith is found in the eagerness that we have to let others have it. The third is the stimulating and encouraging influence of hope. For such a world as ours, we need to maintain every bit of Christian idealism. Hope is the mark of all who are friends of God through Christ. It was a dauntless, pioneer missionary, Adoniram Judson, who said that "the prospects for missions are as bright as the promises of God". We need, however, to remember that there is no such thing as an unconditional promise. It is for us to fulfil the conditions attached to the promises and the promises, exceeding great and precious, will not tarry. Do we really believe that in the Gospel of the Kingdom we have the way to and the power for a righteous and lasting social order?

Making this World Better

NOTHING is more frequently said in our time than that the Church has to take an active, practical interest in all social, economic and political concerns. It is held also that for the greater part of its history Protestantism has declined from the high, exacting, comprehensive standards of its founders, and has distorted its basic doctrine of the priesthood of all believers into an individualism which certainly left the individual with his personal Saviour and direct access to his Saviour but also left him mystified and even unconcerned about the content of social salvation. The inevitable reaction from this has been seen on a large scale in anti-Church or non-religious socialism, though all socialism is not of this character.

The nature of Christian concern for social, economic and political questions has to be carefully defined. It must be something more than the average citizen shows in the affairs of life; otherwise it would be better to drop altogether the adjective "Christian". The very mainspring of Christian concern must be sought in the distinctive teaching of Jesus Christ, arising out of the very wholeness of that teaching, and so having a secure anchorage in the Scriptures. That involves at least two fundamental emphases—that faith is something to be worked out throughout all life, and that it is not possible to have a simple, pure Christianity without its full range of social applications. Too often the Church is tempted to restrict itself to what it calls purely spiritual judgments, and all this may amount to nothing more than an evasion of difficult and complex issues. The Bible speaks of a redemption for man from all the evil of this world, but it is also a redemption which lays upon man a new responsibility for his life in community with others upon this earth.

But there are not wanting in modern times the voices which bid the Church pause and beware of this whole way of presenting the Gospel of the Kingdom. This is usually done by taking a stand upon certain great texts. First, there are our Lord's own words to Pilate, "My Kingdom is not of this world" (John 18, 36). This is interpreted as making it certain that the gulf between essential Christianity and the state of this world is unbridgeable, and that the Kingdom has nothing to do with worldly conditions. But the deeper insight seems to be that Christ is assuring an earthly ruler who understands nothing but worldly ideas and considerations that His Kingdom has its origin in a transcendent world, that its methods and laws are utterly different from those of an earthly empire. That is a grand and utterly secure truth, but it does not imply that the Kingdom has simply nothing to do with this world.

A second passage frequently used in this way is "Love not the world, neither the things that are in the world. If any man love the world, the love of the Father is not in him. For all that is in the world, the lust of the flesh, and the lust of the eyes, and the pride of life, is not of the Father, but is of the world. And the world passeth away and the lust thereof, but he that doeth the will of God abideth forever" (1 John 2, 15–17). These verses must never be dissociated from John 3, 16—"God so loved the world". Obviously they do not mean that we are forbidden to love the world that God so loves. What we are warned against is everything in the life of this world which exists and flourishes in defiance of the good will and loving purpose of God. Three examples are given us—bodily pleasure in all its selfish, sordid and extreme forms, the empty, uppish showiness of life, and vain glory in ways of livelihood. All these include a multitude of sins and belong to the order of things that is doomed to pass away. It must not be overlooked that this very passage occurs in a chapter which has for its leading theme love of the brethren, and that is not possible without a whole range of social applications here and now.

A third text which is drawn into the armoury of those who believe that the Church errs when it speaks in terms of social salvation is "For the Kingdom of God is not meat and drink, but righteousness and peace and joy in the Holy Spirit" (Romans 14, 17). In its context, this does not mean that the Kingdom has nothing to do with our physical needs at all or with a just and secure way of meeting them. It does mean that the life of the Kingdom is far above small details as to what we may eat or drink, and that those who are in the Kingdom have received by the Holy Spirit such accessions of new life and power that they can be considerate of weaker brethren whose conscience may be worried by these smaller matters. The emphasis here is that the life of the Kingdom is such as the world itself knows nothing of and cannot produce, for it is from above for those who are "risen with Christ". The special problem which Paul had in mind here (as in 1 Cor. 10, 31–33; Colossians 2, 16–23; Acts 21, 20–26; 1 Cor. 9, 20) is our Christian responsibility to respect the scruples of others which we do not honestly share and to be watchful for the peace and the building up of the Church. No Christian in any age is likely to suggest that the Kingdom merely means what Kipling once called "the haberdashery of success". Everything in this world which might come under the phrase "meat and drink" is to be held in the Kingdom not in isolation as if nothing else matters, and not in supremacy as if all this was most worth securing. The true citizens of the Kingdom put all this in its right place. They do not hold aloof from it, though they must be willingly detached from it at heart.

Some of the greatest of New Testament scholars in our day have been emphasising that our Lord was guided in His mission by two profound considerations—a deep, full understanding of the Old Testament Scriptures and a sure, penetrating judgment of His own contemporary situation. It cannot be different for His servants and disciples in any age. We can help forward the Kingdom only by a deep understanding of all the Scriptures and by a penetrating judgment of our own age. So we find ourselves made strong with a firm, buoyant resolution to make relevant the truth of the Scriptures to the needs and torments of our age.

Unless the Church deeply feels that the making of a better world is indeed its concern and task; though not its complete concern and task, it should probably have less to say by way of lament for the degeneracy of the times and of complaint because so many in the world seem completely deaf to the Gospel-call. If the Church's message is strictly "redemption from this world", the Church's task could be more clearly defined, and become more definite in a narrow kind of way. But there is so much in the Bible to rebuke us here. To be sure, ours is a time when the hope of transforming this world by the impact of the Gospel seems a very vain hope. The facts of cruel persecution for the sake of Christ in this 20th Century do indeed make us pause when we are tempted to easy optimism. Within living memory the roll of the martyrs has been immensely increased, probably beyond anything that took place in the very worst days of persecution by the Roman Empire. We may well salute the courage and steadfastness of this noble army, but we are left wondering about the prospects of a better world when such things are still possible after all the centuries of Christian teaching and influence. From time to time the world still behaves with criminal cruelty and folly. Nor must we close our eyes to the fact that one of the possibilities before mankind is that envisaged in 2 Peter 3, 7–13—a possibility hitherto held back from fulfilment by the longsuffering of God, but one which evil expressing itself in terms of modern warfare might conceivably bring to pass.

Whether we like it or not, we live in our own time, and we have to hope for a better world in our own time. We are not imprisoned by the character of our times. The Church has to insist that the better world has to come from full Christianity, utterly rooted and grounded in Christ, and not just from human ideas and plans touched and tinged with "the Christian spirit". Secular efforts, even when they have a slight, decorative fringe of Christianity, cannot give us the Kingdom. This is far removed from the true union of the secular and the sacred. Our hopes for the future of mankind have to be supported and nourished by the complete organism of Christian truth as revealed in the Scriptures. To many a secularly-minded reformer and politician this is a most unpalatable morsel. Those who do not believe in Christianity or even in God hold the view that man's problems and tensions can be solved ultimately by better education, more relevant political effort, or a new economic system. But these are no substitute for Christ. All history up till now shows that this cannot be done, that it is not in man by his unaided efforts to direct his steps, and that the event along that road would have to be a universal dictatorship, as in George Orwell's "1984".

Between periodic wars, the nations bend their endeavours to a task of reconstruction—the building of a better world. This has generally been done with the blended emotions of idealism and cynicism. The facts of what has been achieved in this way are impressive, and would be even more so but for the immense, wasteful burden of expenditure on modern weapons. But in all this the seeds of decay and destruction seem to work. It is hard to get people in general to see what the real alternatives are. Over against secular humanism which puts the primary, if not the sole, stress on what man's action can do has to be set the view of the Bible that the supreme factor is God's action to which we respond by faith and obedience. To multitudes the latter seems very vague and worthless in practice. Who will ever state and urge home these alternatives but the spokesmen of the Gospel? Careful and searching study of the Bible is essential for the support of these alternatives, and the Church has to see to it that the fruits of such study are communicated in words that do get home with the people, taking note that "the humanist is seldom at a loss for words".

The purpose of evangelism is the consummation of God's will for all mankind, the establishing of His reign over all life; but the Church cannot but be slack in evangelism if it is not profoundly convicted of God's redemptive purpose for the whole life of the whole world which He created and still sustains. It is a world Christian fellowship we are working for. We have to strive without ceasing for the direct conversion of individuals, but not for that alone. The cry for justice and freedom is as clear and strong in the Bible as the call for repentance. The Church has to be wide awake to big social changes and to be alert to direct them in the light of the truth revealed in the Scriptures. If we must hold to "the radical otherness of the Kingdom" in respect of its source and its final fulfilment, we must equally hold that there are unmeasured new possibilities for this world through the spread and practice of the Gospel. The Church is not intended by its Lord "to be happy to sit in heavenly places behind closed doors", as Dr. D. T. Niles puts it. Certain types of preaching are indeed "pietistically irrelevant", while other types are too similar to topical leading articles in a good daily newspaper. When evangelistic preaching has not the remotest bearing on the problems of the age, the fatal tendency is encouraged of putting religion in one closed compartment and economics and politics and world events in another. Is it really true that, when set in its right perspective, what happens in and to the whole community life of this world is a small thing? If so, the Church should fearlessly say so. But the Church is nearer the truth when it proclaims that "we have hardly yet begun to explore the meaning of a common life ruled by the law of Christ, which is the true fulfilment of human possibility" (F. R. Barry). When a century ago F. D. Maurice wrote "The Church is there to show the world its true centre", he surely meant that the world, in all its societies and nations, cannot hope to bring men to their goal without the instruction, the inspiration and the fellowship of the Gospel. Only so can we hope for the rule of justice, responsibility and love. Many years ago there was a best seller entitled "Praying and Working", now long forgotten, in which the author, Dr. Fleming Stevenson, wrote "There is a Kingdom into which none enter but children, in which the children play with infinite forces, where the child's little finger becomes stronger than the giant world; a wide Kingdom where the world exists only by sufference; to which the world's laws and developments are forever subjected; in which the world lies a foolish, wilful dream in the solid truth of the day". True indeed— so long as this does not move us to carelessness about or despair of the life of this world, but rather to redoubled effort to change its wilful, foolish dream.

2

When the Church was still very young, Peter found it necessary to say that the judgment of God would begin at the house of God (1 Peter 4, 17–18). So it must always be. For the making of a better world, a better Church is the first necessity. The Church, hearing from many quarters "Physician, heal thyself", requires to look inward to its own state, recognising that it is so much less than it ought to be. "The Christian community is neither sufficiently detached nor sufficiently concerned. The Church's perennial failure is to be so identified with the world that it cannot speak to it and to be so remote from it that, again, it cannot speak to it"

(J. A. T. Robinson). On the other hand, the Church often falls into confusion and frustration because it listens overmuch to voices that have little to say or pays excessive respect to those who wish to cling tenaciously to man-made traditions and conventions (Isaiah 29, 13; Mark 7, 6–8), or even because it makes extravagant claims for itself as if God's action were wholly restricted to itself. The Church does not err when it proclaims itself to be the divinely appointed instrument of the Kingdom, and it has usually been careful not to identify itself with the Kingdom. On the vital theme of the relation of the Church's mission and the Kingdom, Karl Barth says "the Church cannot replace or establish the Kingdom; it is the work of God from above, and the Church's mission is obedience to it".

It would be idle and false to belittle the achievements of the Christian Church, especially at its most vital periods and often against fearful odds. The present time is not without its encouraging facts and prospects. However, it still remains true that elements of weakness in the Church are detracting seriously from its immediate influence on the vast masses of people who are outside and reducing its capacity as the instrument of the Kingdom. In many of the older Churches, only a minority of its members are active and interested. Someone has said that a congregation gathering for worship is like a unit of the army going into action, and that absence from worship is like part of the unit running away as they go into action. If that be so, at least half of the members of the Church are in habitual flight, including a considerable proportion of the pledged officers of the army of the Lord who, like the absentee rank and file, made a public vow to be Christ's faithful disciples to the end of their life. The making of the better world is held back above all by the Church's nominal members, men and women who are probably people of their word in relation to their fellows but who seem without scruple or hesitation to be ready to break their word to God.

For those who know the facts, the younger Churches

which have grown up as a result of the modern missionary movement, have their powerful appeal and encouragement. They have shown remarkable resilience and courage in their own missionary outreach; and it is likely that they are to solve some problems sooner than the parent Churches of the West, e.g. the reunion question which is made very urgent for them by the vastness and the urgency of their evangelistic task. But we dare not overlook the facts that these Churches are still a small minority of the population of the lands where they exist, that the old religions are very active nowadays, that these Churches are economically poor and lacking in an adequate supply of trained leaders, that many of their members have no deep grasp or experience of the Christian faith, and that the second and the third generation of Christians often tend to be slack and nominal.

"Too little and too late"—these sad, ominous words are written over large tracts of the Church's history as well as over political history. Only when we are ignorant of the facts are we likely to question this. Although we need to beware of "constructing hypothetical history" in a nostalgic and querulous way, and of spreading gloom by harping too much on the "might have beens", we stand to gain by a frank and loving examination of the Church's strength and weakness. The Christian Church ought to have been instantly alive to the fact that certain conditions which developed in connection with the Industrial Revolution were essentially incompatible with the Gospel, but it was not so. Two great movements like the Wesleyan revival and the Industrial Revolution, not so far separated in time, seemed to by-pass each other, with little mutual relationship and influence. This failure meant the large-scale alienation of the "working class", and the rise of an industrial worker class which has never been within the Church at all to any notable degree. Was the conception of the Gospel in that period too other-worldly? Here is a situation which has affected the task of evangelism for generations, and still does so. In Britain these social conditions have largely been corrected, and indeed radically changed. But this is not so yet on a world scale, in India, the East and in Africa. Does the Church everywhere now recognise that these conditions are incompatible with the Gospel? If not, we are still operating with a partial Gospel.

It is a fact to give us pause that the Churches which have most definitely professed the full, orthodox position in dogmatic theology have on the whole been less active in social concern than say the Unitarian Church which has strong humanitarian principles but is far removed from orthodoxy, or even the Society of Friends which also stands at some distance from orthodoxy. Loyalty to the Bible is sufficient, however, to retain and to integrate both orthodoxy in theology and the principles of Christian action which spring from it. Looking back over a century, we can see that, when all allowance is made for many personal kindnesses to the needy and also for organized, benevolent schemes, strong profession of Christianity was frequently made by men who were also upholders of unjust, cruel social conditions and who themselves benefited greatly by these conditions. At the present time the same phenomenon is tragically evident in South Africa where certain Churches seem to manage to combine widespread, sacrificial zeal in evangelism and mission with the racial policy of apartheid which the Church generally regards as incompatible with the teaching of Christ as to the nature of man. The Church in our time needs to go in for large-scale study of social development in strategic periods, of the kind so well done by Dr. Stewart Mechie, in "The Church and Scottish Social Development, 1780 to 1870". Two lessons clearly emerge—the living conditions revealed in such a study have something very vital to do with the alienation of the masses from the Church, but the Church was not so utterly destitute of concern in these matters as its critics often charge it with being, least of all in its alert, pioneering, prophetic figures.

It is piercingly obvious that the Church is not yet strong enough with the strength that Christ intended, to secure great accessions from the outsiders or to change the nation's ways. This is to be accepted with frankness and humility, not with pessimism and lethargy. A Christian society cannot be reached without Christian worship, but a Church that appears withdrawn from the world or hesitant about involvement in the world is not able to do the proper work of evangelism, to stimulate in unbelieving souls the genuine Christian convictions which lead to Christian worship and action. There is a simple rhyme which enshrines the heart of truth in this regard:

"I sought my soul, but my soul I could not see,
I sought my God, but my God eluded me,
I sought my brother, and I found all three."

When the Churches of the Reformation look back to the movement of four centuries ago which brought them into being, they should be aware that the Reformation had an inward side and an outward—a rebirth of genuine Christian life in the souls of men and a reconstruction of the Church and its worship in the light of that rebirth. But all reforms in the Church's structure and constitution, however important and necessary, are secondary, derivative, and auxiliary. It is not the inefficiencies of organisation or the deficiencies of structure that mainly keep the Church from greater influence. No Reformer ever held such a view, for their chief passion was for inward reform—the new, supernatural life in the soul, the gift and power of the Holy Spirit, a distinctiveness of character marking out the people of God. There has been a widespread revival in recent times of the Biblical description of the Church as "the people of God". It is a great responsibility to stand under such a name. The outsider who considers the matter is puzzled by the title, for he is not able to see much difference between those who use it and those who do not. The people of God have to become more manifestly the people of God. Part of the present weakness of the Church is that such a small proportion of its members are willing to take the necessary steps—regular Bible study, new habits of prayer, working out together the implications of the Gospel for life, venturing out to reach and influence others—by which the Church can develop the resources for the large opportunity and challenge of this century. God is a God of infinite patience, but the people of God are certainly keeping Him waiting and delaying His good purposes for men everywhere. This is our judgment now, beginning at the house of God. The end which God has in view, through judgment and mercy, is "a fair and glorious Church, not having spot or wrinkle or any such thing" (Ephesians 5, 27). The spots on the life of the Church, like spots on the face, are usually produced by impurities in the inward blood-stream. The wrinkles in the life of the Church, as on a human face, are traced by anxiety, tension, or age. Sometimes our tests of what is a flourishing Church are mistaken, because they are just worldly. It depends almost entirely on the quality of life in the members. When on a greatly increased scale Church members welcome every opportunity of worship and attend as frequently as possible and not as seldom as possible, when they do not grudge sacrifice in money, time and work, when they eagerly go out to share with others what they believe, when they know and regularly use the way to go back to God for renewal in sincerity and zeal, the Church will be in a stronger position to speak on what a better world means and to take action towards it.

3

Charles Kingsley, whose writings did so much to bring home to the common people what a deeper thinker like

F. D. Maurice had been teaching on social salvation, held up the Bible as "the true reformer's guide, the true God's voice against tyrants, humbugs and idlers". That same conviction is sufficient to explain why many Christians have earnestly sought to make a Christian testimony affecting every area of life. They have done so at the bidding of their conception of God in Christ as One Who is personally and immediately interested in everything that affects the quality of the life of human beings—family relationship first of all and then all social, political, economic and industrial relationship spreading far beyond the family. To see Christianity and all these spheres drifting further and further apart was a grief to the best Christians of the past, and it ought to be so for us today. They believed that the real roots of democracy and liberty are in God, and that these values are exposed to deadly inward peril if they come to be cut off from their roots, and that this is a more serious danger than attack from outside by those who do not believe in democracy and liberty.

These Christian voices from the past would urge us in our time, when we enjoy the undoubted benefits of the Welfare State, to be vigilant that it too does not get away from a Christian anchorage. The Welfare State itself raises new problems and puts heavy strains on the personal character of all the people in whose hands it is to work it. At these points of tension where the issues are faithfulness and honesty in the quality and spirit of daily work, the Christian anchorage is immensely necessary. Can man get all he wants in the way of economic security and social justice without Christianity? The emphasis of the thinking being done on these matters in the World Council of Churches is that he can not. To separate the Christian religion from all other spheres of man's activity will bring an evil harvest on both sides. The Church may often have to find itself pulling against powerful forces in society. This is unavoidable, for "where no tension exists either the society is regenerate or the Church is conformed"—to quote the World Council report on "The Church and Society". Similarly, the Evanston report proclaims, "Their calling requires Christians to witness to the Kingdom of Christ and the unity of all mankind and to strive through social and political action to secure justice, freedom and peace for all as a foretaste of that Kingdom into which the faithful shall be gathered". A man deeply engaged in Church work and in politics confesses that "to be in politics without the sustaining power of the Holy Spirit and without the constraining love of Christ is to be in a jungle. Motives change as faith declines". He welcomes the reawakened social awareness of the Church and regards the present age as "Christianity's second date with Destiny since Calvary (the first was Constantine's conversion)" (George Thomson. "The Christian Heritage in Politics", 21, 73).

An excellent example of the kind of thinking that has to be done on all these issues is a book by D. L. Munby, "Christianity and Economic Problems". The author is a University teacher of economics, and he also has a thorough grasp of Christian doctrine. His entire argument is lucid, firm, and securely grounded in the twofold understanding of Christianity and the science of economics. It ranges over the complex problems of wealth and poverty, employment, inflation, the price system, the business man in society, the workers and their organisation, state action in the economic scene, and the international scene. At every point an impressive effort is made to bring together the Christian doctrine of man and these economic questions, and it is shown how the working out of the principles governing such an alliance raises not a few painful dilemmas, and that clear-cut directives are not to be expected. But the basic position in this book is that not only the teaching of Christ on the nature of man but the central doctrine of God as Trinity, implies involvement by Christians in the whole material world which God has made to be the present home of man. Jesus Christ has not given His Church a rigid, definite law to govern this or that situation. In this respect He is in line with the

Old Testament prophets who, although they have so much to say in the name of the Lord on social and national affairs, do not present their message as legislators. The teaching of Jesus is new because of its central exaltation of the principle of Love, in an even higher and more exacting form than the Old Testament law—and also it is final because there is nothing higher to exalt that we can conceive. The application of this principle calls for hard thinking and resolute purpose, for the painful dilemmas will always be encountered, e.g. in the pacifist and non-pacifist position, in the attainment of a true equality, and upon occasion compromise with evil may be necessary in our tangled human scene. But this does not mean that Christ's teaching is so idealistic as to be irrelevant, nor that the last word in human affairs rests with an un-Christian pessimism.

The Church cannot be in line with the Will of God if it is content to be a mere spectator of events, still less if it degenerates into playing the role of the protesting, hopeless denunciator of events. Not only must it be confident in the principles which have to be applied, but it has to take a leading part in positive programmes for their application. It is almost universally agreed that great harm can be done if and when the Church becomes the agent of party politics, but short of that there is a part for the Church to play in all social, economic and political affairs. The true interests of the Kingdom may be jeopardized in one or other of two ways—by the Church's unwise and uninformed meddling in these affairs and by the Church's detached abstention from them altogether. In the course of history there is little doubt that the greater danger has been along the latter line, especially when that was dictated, as it normally was, by a distorted comprehension of what the Bible teaches. There are no quick, easy, cut and dry solutions, but there is one sovereign principle of love. To carry that out and to get right in to the many-sided conflict necessary for the carrying of it out, is obedience to the will and purpose of God. For in these matters too there is a way for man to know

God, as a striking passage in Jeremiah says, (22, 13–16)—and this is impressively re-affirmed by our Lord in His exposition of the basis on which man's final judgment will proceed (Matthew 25. 31–46). When He put the question "Man, who made me a divider over you" (Luke 12, 14), He was rebuking a man's covetousness, but He was not proclaiming Himself to be sublimely indifferent to justice in these and all other social concerns of man's life in community. In a recent questionnaire, 56% of those taking part said "No" to the question "Should the Church concern itself with politics?" and 62% said "No" to the question "Should the Church confine itself to spiritual matters and let secular matters stand?" How are these two negatives related? What is the difference between "political" and "secular"? The replies are hard to reconcile, unless "politics" was taken to mean party politics.

It is not too much to say that there is a most important sense in which the Church has to strive to be the true defender of mankind. The Church must have its clear answer, both penitent and virile, to the attack of those in our time who say that the Church has had its chance and failed to use it, that it has had a long innings for nineteen centuries and has little to show for it. These critics have to be instructed in the facts which support the contrary view, and the facts are indeed there; but there has to be no glossing over and explaining away the facts on which the attack is based for they are also there. Meanwhile the Church has to see to it that we leave nothing out that is essential to a complete and obedient presentation of Christ's message to the world. In different ways conservative orthodoxy and liberal humanism left out something essential—the former neglecting what solid obedience to the Gospel means in practice, the latter overlooking the deep power of evil in ordinary people and the eternal nature of the redemption provided in Christ. The Welfare State is not the Kingdom of God. In better living conditions we are still faced with the dark, basic reality of sin, and also with the central question as to what is after all the essential meaning and purpose of man's life upon this earth. It is, of course, always splendidly true that even now Christ reigns in the hearts of those who by faith and surrender have died and risen again with Him; but that does not absolve us from responsibility for seeking a new Christian social order, and from blazing abroad the assurance that there is to be a final victory won by Christ and that all His enemies in this world, or any other world where they may be, have to yield to Him or perish. The Church does indeed urgently require to think out and preach what Dr. Vidler calls "a theology of terrestrial values", "a holy worldliness"—but only a Church deeply aware of its peculiar responsibility for the world is in a position to do so, not a Church holding itself aloof from the world, or seeking a retreat into traditional piety or theological obscurity.

Most Christians probably tend to be surer of their political convictions than their religious ones, and certainly to be surer of them than of the relation and application of their religious convictions to their political ones. Churches have always tended to be too closely integrated with the existing social, economic and political structure, too closely allied to the ruling party, and too little concerned for the sovereignty and the freedom of the Gospel. The more clearly we hear the voice of God, the more insistently we hear the call of the immediate needs of all our fellowmen of whatever country and race and creed. If this be not so, the most likely alternative is that fear and hate, cupidity and conspiracy, malice and falsehood will increase in the human scene. Detached spirituality is not the answer, and this is indeed a real hindrance and embarrassment to the full efforts for the Kingdom. There is a self-centredness embodied in the whole structure of life, and this often remains untouched by the emotionally-charged individualist appeals of evangelism.

The Irish dramatist, Sean O'Casey, makes one of his characters say, "We ought to have as great a regard for religion as

we can, so as to keep it out of as many things as possible".
Over against that we may set the lines of Francis Adams,

> "Take, then, your paltry Christ,
> Your gentleman God,
> We want the Carpenter's Son,
> With his saw and hod."

Thomas Carlyle had made the same point in his letter of 1850 to Joseph Neuberg "I do not find Christ that pound of fresh-butter character which people have made of him", and he goes on to cite the evidence in the Gospels for Christ's turning upside down the existing fabric of society. Behind the two latter quotations there is a searching for a godly materialism as the mind of the Master. In such an age as ours when non-attendance at Christian worship has developed to embrace the majority of the masses, if any progress towards the godly materialism of the Kingdom is to be made, if in other words Christians are to be guided by their Christian principles in their daily "secular" occupations, the laity must face up to the issues as they have seldom done.

The sub-Christian or anti-Christian elements in society, often tacitly and supinely accepted by the Churches as part of the pattern of things, are very serious obstacles to many outsiders. When an outsider becomes a genuine, convinced insider, he is usually ready to acknowledge that these factors are not the only obstacles, and that the inward state of his own life is probably the worst barrier of all. But the Church has to work for the lessening and removal of these obstacles, and one way of doing it is to strive to demolish the false partition between what is sacred and what is secular in this world.

The great Reformers, and notably Calvin, believed that man could only come to the knowledge of God through the Bible, and that the God to be encountered in the Bible is Creator, Redeemer and Lord of all. From such a conception of God it follows that the divorce between the sacred and the secular has nothing stable on which to rest. None of the great prophets of the Old Testament accept it, but strenuously fight against it. One of the prophets usually classed among the minor prophets, though he is a great encourager of the people and has many lovely passages in his small book, states the true point of view in these words—"In that day there shall be upon the bells of the horses, Holiness unto the Lord; and the pots in the Lord's house shall be like the bowls before the altar, yea, every pot in Jerusalem and in Judah shall be holiness unto the Lord of hosts" (Zech. 14, 20–21). Here is a man who is specially concerned with the problem of reconstruction after a period of rain, and he says that in God's plan for a reconstructed world, when the Shepherd-King is victorious, all life will be consecrated, the distinction between sacred and secular done away, for everyone and everything will be sacred. The bells in the place of work, trade and leisure will be as holy as the Church bells. Holiness has to be brought out from the sanctuary to the streets. If it cannot face the climate of the outside world, it is a weakling. Such a Christianity, separate, pale and cloistered, is spiritual invalidism. The Church has to carry out its faith into the rough, hard, exposed places, amid fierce cross currents and storms; and by that the mind of many will be arrested. The bells on the horses will have a converting power even greater than the bells in the temple.

> "Whatever wakes my mind and soul,
> Thy presence is, O God."

When the sacred and the secular are brought together under one holy, loving will, the gap between the natural and the supernatural will thereby be bridged. We may well be afraid of the rising tide of secularism, which denies and ignores the spiritual and transcendent, or leaves it at best as only a sort of optional, decorative fringe around the edges of life that in its main substance is material with an ungodly materialism. An escapist, sanctimonious, and wholly other-worldly Christianity is futile before such a situation.

It is contrary to the intention of God that life should be shattered into fragments and lived in mutually exclusive compartments. God means life to be whole, and this is to be done by the sacred reaching out to, invading and conquering the secular. The view which insists on holding them apart detracts from the very glory of Creation, for God made the material order, the bells on the horses as well as in the temple, the pots as well as the bowls, Monday as well as Sunday; and so the physical and the material can never be alien or unimportant to Him. The more we bring together these two, in a way which does not bring down either of them but exalts both, the more we do justice to the central Christian affirmation of the Incarnation. The body is not a prison or a cage or a filthy stall, but a shrine; and we are summoned to present our bodies and all our daily affairs a living sacrifice, holy and acceptable to God which is our reasonable service (Romans 12, 1). Evangelism which operates with the acceptance of this unholy distinction is distorted and bedevilled from the start. Here too, as at every point, our greatest need is a return to the Bible.

4

Some further thought must now be given to the conception of a Christian civilization, as something that may once have existed but has now largely disappeared, or something that we still hope and expect to be built up in the time before us. This is an elusive and controversial subject. A book of abiding value, out of all proportion to its size, by Professor John Baillie, "What is Christian Civilization?", gathers together in three short, rich chapters the ideas on this subject that must always guide our thinking as we review what Christianity has made of its opportunity hitherto and as we attempt to assess what its future influence may be. A brief summary of Professor Baillie's lucid, cogent and careful argument is now given.

The first use of the word "Christian" (Acts 11, 26) had no reference to a civilization at all, but was the rather scornful name given to a very small minority within a large hostile or indifferent community. But the minority was a recognisable community, and to that extent the use of the term "Christian" did apply to a community and not only to an individual. The small community was held together by its profession of what it resolutely held to be the true religion, whereas it regarded the larger community around it as adhering to a false religion. They believed that the civilization around them was essentially fallen and doomed, and its ruin kept back only by the patience of God. So far as they honourably could, they participated in the life of the world around them, but many of them were prepared to pay the cost when Christian principle forbade such participation. Their real hope lay in the Kingdom of God into which faith in Christ had brought them, "the life of which they already enjoyed by way of foretaste and for whose speedy consummation they eagerly hoped".

In the early stages of the Church's life, although there were many conversions in all ranks of society, there is little evidence of an expectation that the Church would ever grow beyond a minority or ever be the instrument for a radical change of society as a whole. It is probable but not certain that the early Christians believed that the days of all earthly civilizations were numbered and that the end of all things as they had known them was near, because the consummation of Christ's Kingdom was near. History, however, has gone on; and the Christian mission to the world experienced far-spreading expansion. The most impressive fact of history for two thousand years has been the survival and expansion of the Church, in face of much persecution from outside and despite much weakness and apostasy within. And so we have the rise of Christendom, an order of society marked by and in some real way held together by distinctively Christian teaching; and the very rulers of that society were now professed Christians. In such a situation, however, it was easier to be a Christian, and accordingly there was a lowering of the standards of Christian life for many.

When we reach the Reformation, the ideal of its dynamic leaders was that of a Church that should embrace the whole community, with every aspect of life subject to principles derived from the Bible. The Reformers were probably antagonistic to the conception of the Church as a separated sect, keeping as far away as possible from the life of the community. It is all the sadder, therefore, to confess that in four hundred years Protestantism has been prolific of sects with a world-denying emphasis. Also, it has to be admitted that the Reformers' ideal never got very far in actual operation.

Under the tremendous pressure of new forces in the last two centuries, the whole situation has changed. It is indeed an extreme judgment to say that Christendom has disappeared or that Christian civilization has perished. Civilization as we know it today owes more than it may be aware of to its Christian background, in its laws, manners and public standards. Ought the Church now to recognise that it holds "a minority position within a society no longer Christian in any significant sense?" There is much diffused, diluted Christianity around us. Bearing in mind the insidious perils of this condition, must the Church frankly retreat into the remnant position, and so avoid the risk of growing more and more secular-minded itself?

Professor Baillie indicates that his sympathies lie in the opposite direction, as he goes on to examine "the future of the West". Christian belief, with all its teaching about the unity of man, is at the foundation of European civilization at its best; and the importance of this cannot be overestimated. In spite of all the evidence in modern times for a lapsing in society from Christian standards, the general conscience is still Christian, still vitally directed by what Christianity brought into the world. If, however, the modern world attempts to hold on to the Christian moral ideas and practices, but to reject the under-girding Christian beliefs in God and the Redeemer as just "myths", it is only a matter of time until the moral ideas and practices will weaken and fade. "It is unlikely that the Christian conscience of the West can long survive its original setting of belief and its original nourishment of worship". A Christian civilization may then be defined as one in which Christian belief in God, with all its implications for liberty, justice and brotherhood, and all its emphasis on truth, goodness and beauty "sets the tone for society", although many members of that society may not be professing Christians. The picture, however, has always to be completed by the addition of the Biblical emphasis that all earthly civilizations, even the most Christianized we can conceive, fall under the ultimate judgment of God, "for here we have no continuing city".

To this summary of Professor Baillie's book may be added a note on another small book which is akin to it—"The Idea of a Christian Society" by T. S. Eliot, held by many to be the leading British poet of this century. It was written just on the eve of the second World War. It contains a closely-knit, if somewhat circuitous argument, and the characteristic outlook of the very High-Churchman gleams through it. Mr. Eliot is on the whole optimistic, for one of his main positions is that "a society has not ceased to be Christian until it has become positively something else", and he judges that our culture on its positive side is still Christian. He is also quite definite theologically for he defines a Christian society as "a society of men whose Christianity is communal before being individual". This is indeed, in his own words, "large and fundamental", "with practical results that may be inconvenient", something "from which even the majority of professing Christians may shrink, for no scheme for a change of society can be made to appear immediately palatable, except by falsehood, until society has become so desperate that it will accept any change. A Christian society only becomes acceptable after you have fairly examined the alternatives". Towards the end of the book, he states the alternatives—"If you will not have God (and He is a jealous God), you should pay your respects to Hitler or Stalin".

It is unnecessary to follow Mr. Eliot's argument in detail, as he diagnoses the three elements in a Christian society to be a Christian State, a Christian Community and the Community of Christians. These are his minimum requirements, and it is not altogether easy to see them distinctly. But he is practical enough as he considers what these minimum requirements would mean in the realm of education, the arts, economics, and for the organisation and reunion of the Church. He sees the conception of a National Church as dangerous for the Christian society. But his final word on the subject is that "we cannot be satisfied to be Christians at our devotions and merely secular reformers all the rest of the week, for there is one question that we need to ask ourselves every day and about whatever business. The Church has perpetually to answer this question: to what purpose were we born? What is the end of Man?" The complete answer, he would hold, cannot be given within any Christian society realizable here, but equally so it cannot be given in separation from such a society.

The line of thought advocated in these two books is one which the Church ought to pursue with all vigour and hope. There should be a most powerful incentive to this in the twentieth century from the sombre reflection that God found it necessary to permit the rise and spread of Communism because of the slow progress that was being made in the Christianizing of all life. The steady work of the Church down the generations and the special evangelistic missions to which it has given itself from time to time have a notable record of achievement, but on the whole it has not stirred the community, least of all our modern, industrialized society.

We believe that the course of history can be changed in two ways at least—by violent revolution or by the inculcation of right ideas and actions. What the Church has to offer is able to change the world for its lasting good. It would be a sure sign that our Western civilization is becoming more Christian if the Christian countries proceeded to give away large sums for the benefit of the under-developed peoples, even at the cost of a lowering of our own standards of living, and if powerful business firms with Christian leadership that have made enormous profits through war were to renounce these for the common good. Man's achievements have been truly wonderful, and there is much healthy forward-looking in our time. The Church is never under any Divine summons to maintain an attitude of suspicion towards all this or to wage warfare against it. It is called to be at war with all evil in society, in itself and in the human heart. The Church must reject the kind of advice contained in an old Chinese proverb—

> "Don't help on the big chariots,
> You will only get covered with dust;
> Don't think of the world's sorrows,
> You will only be doomed to despair."

The Church is very close to the Scriptures when it teaches that, provided the conditions are accepted, the promises of God will be fulfilled, and that history, "a long-lived storm of great events" is leading to something good. If we hold that a dark force like apartheid is doomed in the last resort, it will not be by political manoeuvre but by the Spirit of Christ. In every direction it is true that falsehood is vanquished only by truth, and for the Christian that means by the moral and spiritual passion of the Gospel. The Church is the bearer and the interpreter to the world of men of the Christian ethic, grounded in the full Christian belief from which it cannot be extricated. It should also be foremost in the ranks of those who work out how these Christian principles can be made to operate—a realm of thought described in our day as "the middle axioms" or "the social strategies". There is much hope in the fact that the number of Christians who believe that concern for the social, economic and political life of God's children is a vital test of a living and obedient Church is growing; and it may well be that those who hold this view now exceed those who do not.

It is as sure as anything can be that the civilization which is fast growing up around us is more and more under the domination of science, and there is now a firm alliance between science and technology. Man is continually seeking out new and marvellous and potentially dangerous inventions. It is generally recognised that there are tendencies in this whole development towards the dehumanizing and degrading of man's life. This has been put facetiously and extravagantly by the man who said "Vacuum cleaners corrupt, washing machines corrupt absolutely"; and the truth that this stands for has to be balanced by the other truth, stated by Professor Gilbert Murray, "the machine is a great moral educator".

The Church has to take note of the tremendous interest of the rising generation in all this realm of scientific knowledge and invention. There can be no turning back of the clock. It is not to be decried or deplored, but welcomed, guided and set in the right framework of the essential Christian doctrines of the nature of God and the nature of man. The Church alone can do this—to show where God comes into it, that all this has not dismissed God, as some think or fear, and that there is a real, limited revelation of God in science as in nature which is the scene of the operations of science, while holding with unabated conviction that the full, saving Revelation of God is in Jesus Christ and none other.

A machine civilization has also to be made Christian, else it will degenerate into a modern idolatory. An Old Testament prophet had a glimpse of what this might be in primitive terms—"Therefore they sacrifice unto their net and burn incense unto their drag; because by them their portion is fat and their meat plenteous" (Habakkuk 1, 16). This is as if we were to offer sacrifices to aeroplanes, electronic reckoners, or hydrogen bombs—which would be the final sacrilege. Man frequently worships what he makes himself, and this is far beyond the worthy and legitimate pride and satisfaction which people ought to have in what they do well for themselves. Man makes his machines out of materials which are given to him by the Creator, and his very knowledge, energy and talents devoted to invention come from the same Source. Man also is tempted to worship what makes him prosperous and comfortable, as the text just quoted emphasizes; and, when that happens, man's true life is being threatened by his own inventions. When properly understood and used, all that man makes and all the prosperity and comfort that follow, should lead his mind and spirit back to God, and convince him that the greatest factors in our complex life are not even the most wonderful things, but human persons. It is along such lines that modern civilization can be made Christian.

5

What can we as Christians hope for in this world? Many are asking that question with deeply anxious tones, and the Church as a whole uses a trumpet with an uncertain sound, and so people are not preparing themselves for the battle. If the Church were confidently and unanimously of the view that there is a hope for the life of mankind upon this earth which belongs to "the very fibre and fabric" of Christ's teaching and that He is indeed the only remedy for the world's manifold discord, there would be an alertness and relevance in evangelism which is often missing.

The most optimistic of the Old Testament prophets is Isaiah. Although he does not hesitate to say that God is to use Assyria, a worse power than Israel, as the rod in His hand to punish Israel, the people of His peculiar choice and of many privileges, he proceeds to say that, when the rod has served its purpose, God will break it (Isaiah 10, 5–20; 14, 24–27). Philistia also is to melt away (Isaiah 14, 28–32); Moab is to be reduced to a contemptible state (15, 1–9); Syria is to be made a ruinous heap (17, 1–3); Ethiopia is to yield up its pride (18, 1–7); and Egypt is to be smitten and then healed (19, 1–19). All these were great worldly powers which resisted God. In some ways the most remarkable prophecy of Isaiah is 19, 23–35. "In that day shall there be a highway out of Egypt to Assyria, and the Assyrian shall come into Egypt, and the Egyptian into Assyria, and the Egyptians shall serve with the Assyrians. In that day shall Israel be the third with Egypt and with Assyria, even a blessing in the midst of the land, whom the Lord of hosts shall bless, saying, Blessed be Egypt my people, and Assyria the work of my hands, and Israel mine inheritance" (cf. 11, 16). Egypt was the ancient enemy of Israel, and Assyria the recent enemy; and they were the two greatest powers of Isaiah's world, at whose hands Israel, the small buffer state, had suffered grievously. But the prophet declares that all this can be left behind. International strife must not have the last word; hostile nations can be made friends, enter into a triple alliance and worship together. He also sees the vision of a whole warless world, with the Lord God supreme over it (2, 1–5). More than any of the other prophets, he saw with crystal clearness that the fulfilment of such hopes had to be associated with the coming of the Messiah (9, 1–7; 11, 1–12).

In the twentieth century, it may seem a mockery even to refer to such hopes, when we know that, on the human side, nothing is holding great nations back from war except the fear of what it would bring to the whole race. Can the hope that is in such passages (and many others in the Old Testament—Isaiah 24, 23; 25, 6-8; 31, 5; 32, 1–8; 40, 5; 49, 6; 51, 3; 54, 13; 60, 1–12; 65, 17–25; Amos 9, 13–15; Hosea 2, 18; Micah 4, 1–7; Zechariah 14, 20–21—not to speak here of the New Testament passages) ever be realized and how? The Bible does not conceal its tensions, paradoxes and seeming contradictions on this issue. It does not allow us to believe that the day will ever come when man will be so naturally good and just that all will come right. It is only by a right-eousness which exceeds the world's that we can hope for a transformation of history, and faith and obedience are the keys. The strong link between the optimistic and the pessi-mistic aspects of the Bible has to be found there. Man is in revolt against the Higher Will, and so human ingenuity and cleverness will never solve the problem. But God has given "exceeding great and precious promises", none of which are unconditional, but all dependent upon faith and obedience. The consummation lies beyond history, but the transforma-tion of history is not excluded.

It is right that we should realise that the judgment of God has fallen upon Christian missions too; but that must not rob us of the hope which lies in the undoubted fact that no religion has become so widespread, so world-wide as Chris-tianity. But the story of the enterprise of Christianity on this earth has been one of ebb and flow, notable advance and disastrous relapse. Something of this is reflected even in the Gospels—"they came to Him from every quarter" (Mark, 1, 45), "the world is gone after Him" (John 12, 19), "many of His disciples went back and walked no more with Him" (John 6, 66), "they all forsook Him and fled" (Mark, 14, 50).

The appearances have often been that Christ is losing ground, and there is much of this sort of evidence today. The Christian missionary has been driven out of China, where one sixth of the total missionary strength of the Churches of the world was at work. It is probable that the total num-ber of missionaries sent out by the Protestant Churches of the world is now under 40,000—about one third less than thirty years ago. Taking a long look back, we can see the stark fact that historic Christianity has never recovered from its greatest setback, the loss of vast territories to Islam, and Islam is still the hardest mission field in the world. Taking a short look around, we note that since the end of the second World War, books have been published with such titles as "France Pagan", "How Heathen is Britain?" "Towards the Reconversion of England". In many lands, the great classics of religion, the Bible, the Analects, the Koran and the Vedic Hymns, have been laid aside for the text-books of science, economics and political theory. There is also a conglomeration of heresies and fancy sects, breathing slaughter against each other. "Humanity has struck its tents and is everywhere on the march" said General Smuts. On the march—whither? To the Kingdom of God?

But there is also an array of facts that encourage. Christ does win a response among people of every culture, creed, colour and class. This is no longer a hope or speculation, but a fact. In every country of the world the Church is present in some organised form, except in Tibet, Afghanistan and Saudi Arabia. Over the earth, the membership of the Christian Church tends to grow. The most pressing political problem before mankind is to find a way of uniting the world. May it not be that God has already pointed the way in the modern missionary movement? There it has been proved that people living in all kinds of conditions, from all kinds of background, with very different economic systems and modes of government, can be brought into a peaceful fellowship with a central allegiance to Jesus Christ. The range of the life of the Church is as wide as the world, and it touches life at every point. The true Church is always "a brotherhood of expectancy".

It is not given to us to know, assuming that the world's life is to be indefinitely prolonged, whether the whole world will ever come to Christ or not. If we did know for certain, the conflicts and setbacks of our time would loom less large and settle into true perspective. But this is a question which admits of neither an easy "Yes" or a final "No". On the one hand, we have the undeniable facts of godlessness and evil, on the other the impossibility of believing that God's purpose could suffer final defeat. Also, it is certain that, if the whole world does not come to Christ, it will never as a whole come to anyone else. The non-Christian religions are experiencing a notable missionary reawakening, but none of them contains such truths on basic questions as will ever fully satisfy the human heart, especially after Christ has been encountered. They too are being shaken by the advance of modern knowledge and by secular attack, and we may well ask what is to happen when the unevangelized areas of the world become industrialized. If the world as a whole is going to have a religious future, it will be a Christian future. In that sense Christ holds the key, and cannot lose that ground.

He has chosen His ground, and will never yield it. He has undertaken nothing that He is powerless to fulfil. He has laid down His own terms and they are never altered. He calls for voluntary decision and free acceptance of an offer that stands open forever. The last word is with Him, and He commands all the horizons. He alone has the answer to the most important question which man can ask "What is our life?" There is no answer just on the natural level, but only one which takes in God, and it is for the world everywhere, to the end of time. Christ holds His ground as the final hope of man. The Bible holds the balance between the conception of a faithful remnant and a vision of every knee bending before Him. As the great missionary historian, Professor Latourette, summed it up "It may be that history will be brought to an end before the community of perfect love, embracing all mankind, will be realised. But if not within history, then beyond it His will will be done in a community perfectly reflecting His self-giving love". At no stage in the long development can the Church reflect her Master's mind except by a lively concern for the world of other people.

It is easy enough to lament the degeneracy of our times, but it would be hard to establish a sure case for the view that the way of life of human beings is certainly getting worse. Much depends on what periods we are comparing, and the dangers of the short view are very great. In the superficial, horizontal sense, the conditions of life have much improved; but in the deep, vertical sense it is very questionable. Is the inward quality and character of life showing improvement? Character is not developed automatically, nor is there a guarantee that one generation can pass it on to the next. Human beings have indeed been likened to heaps of melting snow, in which more and more black spots are coming out. We may have progress in the means of life, without progress in its ends and aims. There is a continual thrust and counter-thrust as between good and evil. Can we be "set free from the bondage of decay to share the glorious liberty of the sons of God?" There is no sense of helplessness in the New Testament. The promise of Jesus Christ to them and to us is "Greater things than these shall ye see; greater things than these shall ye do" (John 1, 50; 14, 12). We have to mark the relation between "see" and "do". Only men who are made better men by God can translate what they see into action.

The better world for which we hope and toil is one which in all its life receives the blessing of God. "Blessing" is one of the very rich words of the Bible, one of the most employed words in Christian worship. It always implies a sense of the favour, the goodwill, the generosity and the approval of God. Frequently it is used in a wholly personal sense— "blessed is the man who trusts in the Lord", "blessed are all who take refuge in Him", "blessed is the man whose transgression is forgiven", "blessed are they that dwell in thy house", "blessed are they who observe justice". But it moves out beyond this to the nation as a whole, "Blessed is the nation whose God is the Lord", and to people who have a special part to play, e.g. Noah (Genesis 9, 1 and 11), Abraham (Genesis, 12, 1–3). It includes material blessings also— long life, a large family, good crops and wealth—especially in the Old Testament. In the New Testament, especially the

Beatitudes, the blessings are those of the Kingdom of God. The Church has always to be on its guard against promoting the idea that blessing and material comfort are joined inseparably by God, as in the mind of the small boy who said "Was it not very nice of God to make our family so rich?" When one of the psalmists declares "I have been young and now am old; yet have I not seen the righteous forsaken or his seed begging bread" (37, 25), a just comment would be that he had not seen very much. A good Christian should be intent on his earthly business and even pray for its increase, like Jabez (1 Chronicles 4, 9–10). But to interpret God's blessing primarily in terms of wealth and comfort is incompatible with the Christian Gospel.

In the better world, under God's blessing, life will be distinguished by four marks. First, there will be in all things a resolute exaltation of truth and reality and a turning away from what is false and sham. Secondly, there will be in public affairs and policies, an over-riding concern for the increase of Christian good. Thirdly, there will be a lifting up of life to higher levels—the human touched with the divine, the temporal with the eternal, man's smallness made big by fellowship with God, and man becoming truly man since he is capable of being the temple of the living God. Fourthly, it will be a world owning the Lordship of Jesus Christ. The significance of the term "Lord" in the Bible is an extensive and complex theme. But the root ideas of the word, the possession of power and authority and rights of ownership, applied sometimes to men and sometimes to God, are associated with Jesus Christ after His Resurrection. God the Father and His Son seek a willing service from men, and have a right to command it, and that covers all life, in a loyal, loving, grateful submission to the Divine Will and Law. In the realm of social salvation too we have to discern the things which can never command the blessing of God, because they are so incompatible with His revealed character and with the Lordship of His Son and with His purpose for His children. In the case of slavery, e.g. it took the Church a long time to see this and the nation a longer time. Individualism never does justice to the rich comprehensiveness of Scriptural truth. The Lordship of Jesus Christ is to be exercised over every part of our personal life, our body, our mind, our spirit, but also over every part of our social life—in the economic, cultural, industrial, political and artistic spheres. In the early Church, "Jesus is Lord" was a sort of rallying-call amid the frustrations and dangers of the time. So ought it to be in modern evangelism.

CHAPTER FIVE

The Kingdom in the New Testament

A GRAVE misuse of the New Testament is made when it is resorted to for a purpose which it is not primarily designed to serve. To treat it as a legalistic handbook of guidance on personal and social conduct, in which we just need to look up the page and quote the text, is an unwarranted practice. Accordingly, there is a danger in selecting one aspect of the teaching of Jesus and treating it as the key to the whole. Nevertheless the conception of the Kingdom comes as near to being the Key element in the New Testament as any that could be named. It is a real, but perhaps over-speculative, question to ask if He would have employed that term, if He had appeared in our day to fulfil His redemptive mission. The vital substance of the message He expressed by that term is unchanging and absolute for all time.

There is no significant difference in meaning between the two phrases "Kingdom of God" and "Kingdom of heaven". Mark, Luke and John always employ the former, Matthew usually the latter, though he too speaks of the "Kingdom of God" (12, 28; 19, 24; 21, 31, 43). Both phrases are closely connected with the idea of eternal life. Jesus of Nazareth took up the call which had been sounded by John the Baptist, "Repent, for the Kingdom of heaven is at hand" (Matthew 3, 2). There is a real continuity between John's mission and Jesus' mission. This was recognised even by Herod who thought that Jesus must be John come back to life again (Mark 6, 14–16). Also, when Jesus wanted to find out from His disciples whom the people thought Him to be, the first reply was "John the Baptist" (Mark 8, 28). Having in the temptations in the wilderness rejected three false methods of fulfilling His mission, He returns with His own resonant call "The time is fulfilled, the Kingdom of God is at hand; repent ye and believe the Gospel" (Mark 1, 14–15). This is after the imprisonment of John; and in Galilee where John had probably never been. The parables which account for one third of His recorded teaching deal, explicitly or implicitly, with the Kingdom. In several cases the parables begin with the words "The Kingdom of God is like. . . ." seed growing secretly, mustard seed, leaven, a great feast, tares, hidden treasure, a costly pearl, a drag-net, a forgiving servant, labourers in the vineyard, ten virgins. The appeal of the penitent thief on his cross envisages a Kingdom of Christ (Luke 23, 42). It was for the Kingdom that He laid down His life (John 18, 33–38).

The charge of His Jewish enemies was that He made Himself a King (John 19, 12), although He had resisted such a proposal as wrong (John 6, 15). But He is King of the new and true Israel. In that sense only could He accept the tumultuous welcome of the crowd on Palm Sunday. "Blessed is the King that cometh in the name of the Lord" (Luke, 19, 38; cf. Psalm 118, 26). It is as King, also, that He conducts the last Judgment (Matthew 25, 34, 40).

In the Epistles, the phrase is used infrequently—Romans 14, 17; 1 Corinthians 4, 20; 6, 9–10; Ephesians 5, 5; 2 Thessalonians 1, 5; Colossians 4, 11; and in these cases the emphasis is on the kind of character required for the life of the Kingdom. In 1 Corinthians 15, 23–24, there is a distinction between the Kingdom of Christ and the Kingdom of God— the Kingdom of Christ having its inauguration at the Resurrection, and pointing forward to the final consummation when God will be all in all. In Acts again the references are few. We are told that in the forty days after His resurrection, Christ spoke to His disciples of "the things concerning the Kingdom of God" (Acts 1, 3), which can only mean His characteristic teaching now set in the light of Calvary and the Resurrection, with Ascension close at hand. The disciples even then did not fully understand, and were thinking in terms of a restored Kingdom of Israel (Acts 1, 6–7), and had to be told that it was not for them "to know the times or the seasons, which the Father hath put in his own power". The main burden of Paul's preaching at Ephesus and Rome (Acts 19, 8; 28, 31) is the Kingdom; and from an earlier reference (14, 22) we learn that Paul taught that men enter the Kingdom by great tribulations.

The New Testament doctrine of the Kingdom has a distinct and even necessary Old Testament background. When Israel, the chosen and covenanted people of God, decided to have a king, there were penetrating, prophetic voices who regarded it with deep distrust. They held that it reduced God's people to the level of the other nations round about, that it was virtually an act of apostasy from their allegiance to the true king, and that it would cost them dear. This view of the kingship is enshrined in 1 Samuel 8, 1–22; 10, 17–25. But that was not the only view of the situation, and the opposite view is stated in 1 Samuel 9, 1–8, 10–27; 10, 1–7, 9–16; 11, 1–11, 15. In terms of the latter interpretation the wellbeing of the life of the nation is bound up with the life of the king, "the lamp of Israel" (2 Samuel, 21, 17); and it was believed that there was a very close relationship between the earthly and the Heavenly King, as in Psalm 89. But the period of the undivided Kingdom was short-lived, covering the reigns of Saul, David and Solomon, less than a century. The subsequent fate of the small kingdoms of Israel and Judah would certainly be associated in many deeply religious minds with what they held to be the original, calamitous mistake of turning away from trust in the Sovereign King.

Under the influence of the great prophets, the idea of a localized God who was sovereign only over his own territory was broken down; and more and more it came to be taught that the God who had chosen Israel was the only true and living God who in due time would assert His sovereign rule over all peoples of the world. This appears clearly in Psalms 72 and 74—"God is my King of old working salvation in the midst of the earth" (74, 12); "God is the King of the whole earth; God reigneth over the heathen; God sitteth on the throne of His holiness" (47, 7–8). Micah looks forward to the time when all nations shall come to the house of the Lord (4, 1–2). In Isaiah above all are the great passages, 9, 1–6; 11, 1–10; 25, 4–5; 65, 17–25. The same conception appears in Psalm 103, 19; 145, 11; 113, 1–5; 22, 23–24; 86, 9–10. The Book of Daniel belongs to the apocalyptic type of literature rather than to the prophetic, and the two great passages in it are 7, 1–18; 12, 1–4—"his dominion is an everlasting dominion, and his Kingdom that which shall not be destroyed". The hearts of faithful people can indeed be lifted up, even in very bad times—"The Lord is King, be the people never so impatient; He sitteth between the cherubim, be the earth never so unquiet" (Psalm 99:1). He will be "King for evermore" (Psalm 10:16; 146:10). In the great code of Deuteronomy we have a remarkable attempt to work out in detail what like society might be if the rule of God was accepted and obeyed. The total impact of Old Testament teaching is that God is to be King over all the nations—the same all-embracing idea as Jesus Christ had in mind when He said that the field for the seed of the Gospel is the world (Matthew 13, 38).

The Kingdom, in the Old Testament, is to come by the direct agency of God, and through a Messianic Person. This hope for a "Redeemer-King" appears only in Israel, not in Egypt or Babylon. It will be most personal, most mysterious, and most comprehensive. But much is said in the Old Testament of the reasons why the Kingdom of God is retarded and its appearance not more evident before the eyes of men. The blessings of the Kingdom are held back by God Himself, even though it would be a delight for Him to bestow them, because the people are unwilling, faithless and disobedient. It is not that in some impenetrable fashion God is reluctant or capricious, for the responsibility lies all the time at man's door. This indeed is one of the few structural ideas that hold the Old Testament together, and Jesus did not come to destroy that, but to confirm and fulfil it. The New Testament Israel, like the Old Testament Israel, is called to live under the Kingship of God; and it is the purpose of Jesus, as the Perfect Revealer of God and the only Redeemer of mankind to make the experience and the laws of the Kingdom manifest to all peoples of the earth. He too would agree with the twofold emphasis of the Psalms—"The Lord reigneth, let the earth rejoice"; "The Lord reigneth, let the people tremble" (Psalms 97, 1; 99, 1). The time to which the whole Old Testament looked forward had come—the decisive hour had struck. In the two or three centuries immediately prior to the birth of Christ, there had been much speculation and writing by the authors of the apocalyptic books which fill up the period between the Testaments. In these works the hope of the Kingdom tended on an increasing scale to be exclusively nationalist, but Jesus broke away from these limitations and fetters, and spoke a word, the same word, to all nations—and the essence of that word was trust in and obedience to the King of heaven and earth.

2

The entire New Testament proclaims with one voice that something utterly new, incomparably splendid and eternally important entered our world in Jesus Christ. "A great redemptive transaction was being effected by God in the Son of Man's generation". This is the reign or rule of God—"the undisputed sovereignty of God throughout His creation" (G. F. Moore). A most marked feature of modern New Testament scholarship is the emphasis on the idea of the Kingdom as already come, although it still remains the duty and the privilege of Christians to pray for its fuller coming. The coming of the Son of Man and the coming of the Kingdom are identical in meaning. This conception of the Kingdom as being now here, since Christ has come, is basic to Professor C. H. Dodd's book "The Parables of the Kingdom". "The Kingdom of God has come upon you" (Matthew 12, 28); "The time has arrived, the Kingdom of God has drawn near" (Mark 1, 14–15); "If I by the finger of God cast out demons, then the Kingdom of God has come upon you" (Luke 11:20). "Blessed are the eyes that see what you see; for I tell you that many prophets and kings desired to see what you see, and did not see it, and to hear what you hear and did not hear it" (Luke 10, 23–24). It is precisely because He has brought the Kingdom that He claims to be greater than Solomon, or Jonah, or the Temple (Luke 11, 31–32). The law and the prophets were until John the Baptist but now the Kingdom has come (Matthew 11, 12–13; Luke 16, 16), and people are forcing their way into it. In Professor Dodd's words "The Kingdom of God, the hope of many generations, has at last come. It is not merely imminent; it is here. The absolute, the "wholly other", has entered into time and space. The sayings which declare the Kingdom to have come are explicit and unequivocal".

One of the very difficult sayings of Jesus about the Kingdom is that spoken after Peter's confession at Caesarea Philippi, "There are some of them that stand here who will not taste of death till they have seen the Kingdom of God come with power" (Mark 9, 1). This cannot be a reference to the Second Coming, for in that case they are not true and Jesus would be in error. They do refer to the gigantic events soon to take place, in the Resurrection, the Ascension and the gift of the Holy Spirit. When the disciples have passed through these experiences, they will know that all the time the Kingdom had been with them in the ministry of their Master in Galilee and Judea. Moreover, this Kingdom has been prepared from the foundation of the world for those accounted worthy to enter it (Matthew 25, 34). In His great Prayer on the eve of Gethsemane, Jesus said two amazing things about the love of God—that the Father loved Him before the foundation of the world, and that the Father loves us with the same love as He loves His Son (John 17, 23–24). To make all that our own in adoring faith and gratitude is to be in the Kingdom. Such a Gospel has to be given to all peoples to hear; He must press on to the "other cities" (Luke 4, 43).

John the Baptist played a big part in God's unfolding purpose, and Jesus paid a remarkable tribute to him when He said that "a greater than John the Baptist had not been born of woman" (Matthew 11, 11)—almost unbelievably remarkable when we remember that Abraham, Moses, David, Amos, Hosea, Isaiah, Jeremiah and the Psalmists had all lived and died before John. But Jesus goes on wistfully to say "notwithstanding he that is least in the Kingdom of heaven is greater than he". In some sense John was outside the Kingdom whose near approach he preached. His conception of repentance was not as deep as that of Jesus. His presentation of godliness was more negative than that of Jesus. He spoke overmuch in terms of Law, and too little in terms of Grace. Like Jesus, he emphasized judgment, but it was scarcely a judgment that was an expression of Love. John certainly pointed out the clear way of duty, but he had little to say on the source of encouragement and inspiration for the doing of it. John was an aloof ascetic, Jesus was not, and John's was not the way of life for the Kingdom. John seemed to wait for the people to come out to him, but Jesus went everywhere to seek them. Yet it was this John of whom Jesus said "he was a burning and a shining light" (John 5, 35). He also told His accusers that if they had understood John, they would have understood Him (Mark 11, 27–33).

The thought of the Kingdom as a present reality is a great and true thought, but it should not be held to exclude the other thought that, as the sovereignty of God comes to be better acknowledged (surely one of the great ends of the

Christian mission), there can be and should be an advance towards a universal sovereignty, general obedience to a universal will. Jesus could hardly exclude this hope without separating Himself from the great prophets. He worked and commands His Church to work for the overcoming of disobedience which is enmity to God. We do not know for certain that man will ever own the true and fruitful allegiance to God rather than the false and fruitless allegiance to evil. Jesus once said that a certain scribe was "not far from the Kingdom" (Mark 12, 34), and the reason for that compliment was the scribe's discreet answer about what matters most in living. Meanwhile it is the responsibility of the faithful minority to exemplify the teachings of the Kingdom. So it was in Elijah's day (1 Kings 18, 20–22); and so too it was for "the saints of the Most High" in Daniel 7, 18, who shall possess the Kingdom forever. Christ has every right to ask of the citizens of the Kingdom obedience, loyalty and trust, for He submitted Himself wholly to that discipline—"though He was a Son, yet learned He obedience by the things which He suffered". (Hebrews, 5, 8). The Kingdom is the fellowship of those who accept what Jesus offers in grace and who submit themselves to the discipline of His yoke (Matthew 11, 27–30).

In the teaching of Jesus there is no distinction between King and Father. The reign of God is a Father's reign. "I thank thee, O Father, Lord of heaven and earth" (Matthew 11, 25). The whole universe is sustained because a Supreme Person whose nature is Holy Love is on the throne. The Father-King is the actual giver of all life and has a continual concern for our true life. There are foreshadowings of this too in the Old Testament. For Jesus Christ, however, the completest title for God is Father, and it had not been so before. No one could have written what Paul writes in Romans 8, 12–39 before the coming of the Kingdom in Christ. But there are anticipatory intimations of this in Old Testament passages which deal with God's care for His children and His expectation of their loving and loyal response, as well as in the other passages where He is represented as the Father of the nation (Psalm 103, 13; Hosea 11, 1–3; Deuteronomy 1, 31; 8, 5; 14, 1; Isaiah 1, 2; 63, 16; Jeremiah 3, 19; Malachi 1, 6; 2, 10; 3, 17). In the Old Testament there is scarcely a trace of radical unbelief in the sense of reasoned questioning as to the existence of God or of His character as Father-King. The only kind of atheism which existed among His people was practical, not theoretical, atheism—the foolish denial in life of the presence of God, the manner of living as if He did not exist. This is probably the reason why one Psalm is given twice—14 and 53, describing the behaviour of the fool who says in his heart that there is no God.

The sovereignty and the almightiness which God has resides in and expresses His Holy Love. Any conception of omnipotence which strays away from Holy Love is misleading, and may indeed involve a denial of the very character of God. This important point is conserved in the Apostles' Creed when it starts with belief in "the Father Almighty" not "the Almighty Father". In the Lord's Prayer the name which is to be hallowed is "our Father which art in heaven". In Christ the Kingdom is essentially a Kingdom of grace, though that phrase is not used in the Gospels. The good news of the Kingdom is that God is mercifully pleased to receive back sinners, His wandered children, by adoption again into His home and family. His relationship to Israel as the chosen people was one of adoption (Exodus 4, 22; Jeremiah 31, 9). Equally so, His relationship to the members of the new Israel is one of adoption. The classic passage here is Romans 8, 14–17—it is by adoption that the bondage of fear is broken, and we are given a new, wholly undeserved, right to enter our true inheritance, "heirs of God and joint heirs with Christ"—breath-taking and almost incredible words.

In his definitive book "The Teaching of Jesus", Professor T. W. Manson raises a point of distinction in Jesus' usage of the term "Father" before and after Peter's great confession at Caesarea Philippi. In a most careful, detailed examination of the texts, he points out that in Mark all the cases of the use of "Father" fall after Peter's confession. In the source known as "Q", the same situation is found; and in both Mark and "Q" the use is in Jesus' prayers or His conversations with His disciples. In Matthew, nearly half the cases are in the Sermon on the Mount, usually regarded as a composite document; otherwise the references in Matthew are also after Peter's confession; and similarly in Luke with the one exception of 2, 49. The four parables which directly teach the Fatherhood of God (Mark 12, 1–11; Luke 11, 11–13; Matthew 21, 28–31; Luke 15, 11–32) all follow Peter's confession. Also, the use of the title "Son of Man" for Himself belongs to this period, and after Peter's confession He speaks of "entering" the Kingdom rather than "the Kingdom has come". It is hardly possible to resist the conclusion that what took place at Caesarea Philippi was a great watershed in the life not only of the disciples but of Jesus also. He is now closer to them than ever, and this finds utterance in the term "Father", and the reason why He is closer is that He has drawn from Peter (speaking for the others as well as himself) the confession that He was the Messiah. From that point onwards He can ask from them a loyalty of a kind hitherto associated with God, and He can disclose to them the dark and unwelcome secret that this loyalty will involve the Cross for Him and for them. "It is not too much to say", Professor Manson sums up, "that Peter's inspired declaration at Caesarea Philippi has changed the whole course of the world's history".

In the closing days of his life, Jesus, knowing that His Passion was near, makes a continual use of the term "Father". We have much evidence of this in John's Gospel—10, 15–17; 10, 29–30; 12, 24–28; 13, 3; 14, 2–3, 6–14, 21–24; 15, 7–9, 15, 16, 23; 16, 15–16, 32; 17, 1–6, 11, 24, 25; 18, 11—but also in the Synoptics, Matthew 26, 29, 39, 53; Mark 14, 36; Luke 22, 29–30; 23, 34, 46. In every case, He is speaking out of deep experience—the experience which at an earlier stage He had expressed in the words preserved in "Q", but so akin to John, "all things are delivered to me of my Father, and no man knoweth the Son but the Father, neither knoweth any man the Father, save the Son, and he to whomsoever the Son will reveal Him" (Matthew 11, 27). This is the kind of isolated verse, in substance and spirit very close to Caesarea Philippi, and yet appearing before it, which is a little difficult for Professor Manson's interpretation, significant and searching as that interpretation is. As Jesus looked out upon life around Him, in the confidence that God was Father-King, He saw the signs of that in all the works of creation, even the most ordinary, the flowers, the grass and the sparrows; and He saw it also in the unfailing, Divine generosity by which the sun shines on the evil and the good, and the rain falls on the just and the unjust.

The main instrument of Jesus' teaching was the parable. By His interpretation of His parables, to them the disciples are let in to "the mystery of the Kingdom" (Mark 4, 11)—and this normally means some aspect of the reign of the Father-King which had not been revealed to men before Christ came. But it is equally clear that we have to understand the miracles of Christ in relation to the Kingdom. They are the evidence of His successful encounter with the powers of evil. He is set against everything in the present world-order which is in defiance of the will and purpose of the Father-King. "Heal the sick" is an essential part of His charge to His disciples as they go out to preach the Kingdom (Matthew 10, 7–8); and newness of health is evidence that the power of the Kingdom is present and being used. It is important that this aspect of the Kingdom should be kept in the Church's view, but not exaggerated as if it were the crowning evidence of the presence of the Kingdom. There is no support in the Gospels for the notion that all sickness, pain and death will ever be completely left behind in the earthly state—that is for the new age in the new world beyond history (Revelation 21, 4–5). Yet Jesus, despite all his unwillingness to give signs and His fear of being regarded as just a wonder-worker, did interpret His miracles as pointers to the Kingdom, outward manifestations of the power of His message and vindications of it (Matthew 11, 4–6; 12, 28; Luke 10, 17; 13, 10–17; Mark 5, 22–43; Luke 7, 11–17; John 11), and also as fulfilment of Old Testament prophecies of what the Messiah would do (Luke 4, 16–20). Some miracles He refused to do, when they were mere portents and prodigies of no worth to anyone. But at the bidding of great compassion for sufferers, He was prepared to use His power as the Divine Son to relieve need and to increase joy and hope. His miracles were done by faith, and scholars have reverently sought to trace how this faith developed in His spiritual pilgrimage from early years. In this whole field of miracle, we are in the presence of the supernatural, a region in the understanding of which we need good guides. Probably the three most penetrating books on the subject for the last half century are "Redemption from this World" by Andrew G. Hogg; "The Faith that Rebels" by David S. Cairns; and "The Miracles of Christ" by John H. Best. When the time is fulfilled, there are miraculous accompaniments, not only in Christ's own generation, but for all generations until the "end" comes.

The reasons for the delay in the more manifest appearing of the rule of the Father-King in the New Testament are fundamentally the same as in the Old Testament, only they take on a more serious aspect because they amount to unbelief in and disloyalty to the Messiah who has now come. All the powers of the supernatural order were now accessible in Christ, but again on the human side there was a disastrous ignoring of the decisive events and a fatal blindness as to their purpose. In Dr. Hogg's words, "the incredible obstinacy of human distrust needlessly prevented what really might have taken place"—and it does so still. God has apparently from the beginning subjected Himself in this matter to the limitation of the uncertain response and the variable character of man. The reign of God is indeed an unchanging and irreversible fact, but there was no general acknowledgment of it. Failure to acknowledge it is loss and ruin—"Woe unto thee Chorazin, woe unto thee Bethsaida"

(Luke 10, 10–14)—"notwithstanding be ye sure of this that
the Kingdom of God is come nigh unto you"—the Kingdom
whose primary summons to repentance and faith had gone
unheeded. The people of His generation had behaved like
sulky children, responding neither to the Baptist's call nor
to Jesus' call (Matthew 11, 16–19). The parable of the Sower
makes it clear that everything depends on the difference in
the soils, for the same good seed is sown everywhere, and
never without good results alongside the poor and negative
results. The only way of "looking for and hasting unto the
coming of the day of God" (2 Peter 3, 12) is to proclaim
everywhere the Gospel of the Kingdom, and the precise
character of that day will depend upon how much harvest
has been reaped and can be reaped in the life of this
world.

When Jesus Christ employed the ideas of the Suffering
Servant and Son of Man to define His Person and mission,
He was making it clear that the Kingdom necessarily involved sacrifice and suffering for Himself and for all His
disciples. The cost of discipleship is stressed more and more
after Caesarea Philippi. The claims which He makes upon
the members of the Kingdom are now seen to be supreme
and absolute—and they are stated in terms of the cross-
bearing involved in following Him. As already pointed out,
there is only one saying of Jesus which, in slightly different
form is found six times in the Gospels—"Whosoever shall
save his life shall lose it and whosoever will lose his life for
my sake shall find it" (Matt. 10:39, 16, 25; Mark 8:35;
Luke 9:24; 17, 33; John 12:25). In the context, cross-bearing
is not carrying our share of the inevitable burdens and mis-
fortunes to which all men in this world are liable—what
Shakespeare calls "the slings and arrows of outrageous fortune", "the thousand natural shocks that flesh is heir to".
It is rather the willing acceptance of the sacrifice and suffering that we could escape, were we not loyal disciples of
Jesus Christ within His Kingdom. For Christ Himself the
suffering was involved in His application of God's merciful,

generous, patient love, in a life of service without parallel before He came and never again to be equalled. This was indeed the reign of the Father-King. God is always seeking to assert His rule in the entire length and breadth and height and depth of human experience, and not merely in detached segments of it. The disciples may not have understood all that it would mean for them when they declared that they were able to drink of the cup that He would drink and to be baptized with the baptism that He was to be baptized with (Mark 10, 35–40). He had told them not to fear those who kill the body (Matthew 10, 28), and it would seem that He did not exclude the possibility of some of His disciples dying with Him at Jerusalem. It is an interesting and significant fact that the Pharisees did not call for the death of some of His followers as well as His own. Part of the suffering of the Kingdom is the family strife which may be involved in obedience to Christ (Luke 12, 49–53). The parable of the Wicked Husbandmen (Mark 12, 1–12) holds together the two main points of the suffering of the long prepared-for Son and the consequent punishment of those responsible for it. The weeping of Christ over the Jerusalem which has now lost its chance is deeply kindred to this parable (Luke 19, 41–44; 13, 34–35).

3

The most reliable way of understanding all that is implied in the New Testament teaching on the Kingdom is to see that it is integrated with all that the Bible teaches on God's ways with and purposes for sinful men. When that is done, three great elements in its meaning stand out—immediate personal inwardness, final vindication and effectiveness in the historical here and now so long as history lasts.

When believers enter into a right relationship with God in Christ, they have entered the Kingdom. On this aspect of it, a most important passage is Luke 17, 20–21, "The Kingdom of God cometh not with observation; neither shall they say, Lo, here! or, lo, there! for, behold, the Kingdom of God is within you". It may well be that the strictly correct translation of the closing phrase is "among you"—but that does not exclude the personal significance of what happens "within" us. From the basic fact that the Kingdom has come among men in Christ, it is only a step, and a necessary one, to proceed to what that means within the individual's life. By our faith we secure for ourselves a part in what is supremely good, true and real. This is the truth enshrined in the parables of the hidden treasure and the costly pearl, although they also teach two contrasted ways of securing it.

The Kingdom of God is something to enter—and this responsibility for entering into a Kingdom which has already come is the main burden of Christ's later ministry, and is seldom heard of in His earlier ministry. The Kingdom becomes in a new sense an immediate, personal reality, for those who have taken the steps to enter it. Those who enter the Kingdom exert an influence in the world, such as is described in the parables of the Seed growing secretly and the Leaven. A true disciple of Christ has thereby made a personal entrance into the Kingdom. The life of the Kingdom is the new life in the individual soul which has surrendered to Jesus Christ, and is nourished in and by the fellowship of kindred souls in the Church. The Church is not just to be identified with the Kingdom, but it is intended to be the society where the laws and principles of the Kingdom are most evident, and engaged in a warfare of love against the powers which are hostile to God. Unfortunately, the words of a vigorous hymn are as yet far from true—"like a mighty army moves the Church of God". The Church is the Kingdom at war, but the decisive battle has been fought and won at the Cross, and the time must come when Christ shall subdue all enemies and hand over the Kingdom to God. The

Church, therefore, must be a fellowship of sacrifice. We have already seen how that was emphasized in the closing stages of Christ's ministry. At the very end, Peter offers to go with Christ even to death (Mark 14, 26–31); and Christ does not forbid Peter or any of the others to do this. We can never build a secure argument on silence, and so we must not make too much of the fact that Jesus does not forbid Peter. On the other hand, we have no reason to suppose that God's purpose for the future of His Church would have been frustrated if some of the disciples had died with their Master, for we must not limit the power of the Kingdom which was released by the triumphant act of God in the Resurrection. Moreover, it is always true that "the sufferings of this present time are not worthy to be compared with the glory that shall be revealed in us" (Romans 8, 18). "For our light affliction which is but for a moment worketh for us a far more exceeding and eternal weight of glory" (2 Corinthians 4, 17). This is more than a promise of compensation; and yet it is not wrong "to have respect unto the recompense of the reward" (Hebrews 11, 26).

This emphasis on the inwardness of the experience of entrance into the Kingdom presupposes that we take with full seriousness the teaching of Christ to the effect that it is already present, and that our eyes have been opened to all that entered our world in the Person of Christ and that in the events of His life, death and resurrection, the decisive hour for mankind is passed. All this holds together with the experience of the reign of God within ourselves, when we have entered into His love; and so we are no longer spectators of the Kingdom but participants. Experience of this kind is made possible only by the Divine generosity, the grace of the Father-King, (Matthew 20, 1–16). This parable of the Labourers brings out as its ruling thought the exceeding kindness of God who calls into His full fellowship those who have no claim upon it at all, and who give up all thinking in terms of what they deserve.

The inwardness of our life in the Kingdom, as personal

response to Jesus Christ, is taught by such passages as Matthew 12, 18; 21, 31; 25, 34; Mark 10, 15; Luke 12, 32; 16, 16; John 3, 3; 10, 10; 18, 36; Romans 14, 17; 1 Corinthians 4, 20; 6, 9–10; Ephesians 5, 5; 2 Thessalonians 1, 5. In John's Gospel the only direct reference to the Kingdom is in 3, 3 "except a man be born again, he cannot see the Kingdom of God" and that could not be surpassed as a statement of the importance of the right inward relationship. In Galatians 5 Paul is giving a detailed statement of what life in the Kingdom means. All Christ's teaching of a Love which reaches sinners and moves them to penitence and consecration illumines the life of the Kingdom in a special way. Above all, the parables of the lost sheep, the lost coin and the lost son, reveal a Love which seeks us as individual persons, seeks before we repent and loves us when our back is turned against it. The big fault of the elder brother was that his attitude to the offender was incompatible with the life of the Kingdom. On the other hand, the outcasts and socially-impossible people might find their way in before the Pharisees—for God does not deal with us on a basis of strict justice, which would leave us all in hopeless darkness (Matthew 23, 13; 21, 28–31). To miss the experience of life in the Kingdom for the sake of increased worldly gain is the sin of the rich fool (Luke 12, 16–20). All Jesus' teaching on personal goodness, work, possessions, family and neighbours, belongs to the way of life which is distinctive of His Kingdom. The Kingdom has its characteristic responsibilities and rewards, and in the parable of the Talents (Matthew 25, 14–30; Luke 19, 12–27), spoken to those who supposed that the Kingdom would immediately appear, we are vividly reminded that the Father-King will call us to give account. We are also warned of the danger of hearing and hearing, and seeing and seeing, and yet not hearing and seeing so effectively as to enter the Kingdom, remaining deaf all the time to the urgent call and blind all the time to the glory of the Kingdom (Isaiah 6, 9–13; Matthew 13, 13–17; Acts 28, 25–28). Fitness for the Kingdom requires a new sense of the priorities of life and of the necessity for constancy and perseverence, as Christ reminded three unsatisfactory candidates for discipleship (Luke 9, 57–62). The only way to learn "the mystery of the Kingdom" is the way in which the disciples learned it, by living with Christ, "in Christ", as Paul would say. It is to people who have entered into this new inward relationship that the mystery is steadily unfolded, and that is not given to anybody who is determined just to speculate and argue and apply irrelevant tests which are mostly drawn from the world of science. The Kingdom which in its perfection is seen in Jesus can and must be seen in measure in His true and faithful followers of every age. "Disciples are apprenticed to the Kingdom of God by living with Jesus".

4

The second main strand in New Testament teaching on the Kingdom is nowadays described by the much-used, perhaps over-used, word "eschatological". The root meaning of that word is that there is an end, a goal, a climax beyond earthly history—a supreme and final consummation in a realm appropriate for such an eventuality in a way that no earthly state could ever be.

It cannot be held, on any just and balanced estimation of the Scriptural evidence, that Jesus believed that this world is so incurably bad and already so deeply alienated from God that it is beyond any doubt heading to ultimate destruction. But He had a settled belief in a great consummation in the future, and much of the language He employed conveys the idea of a sudden, miraculous manifestation of the Kingdom—"a shining out" when men, busy about their worldly activities, have no thought of it happening. And so

He presses home the necessity for preparedness and vigilance for its coming. In the mind of Jesus there was no contradiction between this and the other claim which He made and which was involved in His very Person that the Kingdom had already come. The Father-King, in His own time and way, would establish His reign in a complete and final fashion. He who is the Divinely-sent Founder of the Kingdom is also the Herald of its ultimate completion, and its Agent too. "I beheld Satan as lightning fall from heaven" (Luke 10, 18)—that is His swift and prophetic reaction to the encouraging report of the Seventy that even the devils were subject to them through His name. Not only was their immediate mission successful in a way that gladdened His heart, but He sees beyond it to what it at last signifies, the total downfall of evil. "The Son of Man shall send forth His angels, and they shall gather out of His Kingdom all things that offend, and them which do iniquity. . . . Then shall the righteous shine forth as the sun in the Kingdom of their Father" (Matthew 13, 41–43). When confronted with Christ, the evil powers themselves fear and even realise that He has come to destroy them (Mark 1, 24–26).

Long before the coming of Christ, the Old Testament, in a book where the horizon of thought is singularly wide, stated the fundamental distinction between the hidden and the revealed things of God—"The secret things belong unto the Lord our God, but those things which are revealed belong unto us and to our children forever, that we may do all the words of this law" (Deuteronomy 29, 29). Since Christ has come, the area of the revealed things has been immensely increased—things which man could never by his own searching discover, but they are now disclosed once and for all in Christ. There are at least four of these truths—that a Supreme Person whose nature is Perfect Love is in command, that the way of Salvation for all mankind is in Jesus Christ alone, that God is continually at work bringing into being persons who are fitted by His grace to share His eternal Kingdom with Him, and that God is irrevocably resolved to destroy the realm of evil. That fourth conviction of revelation is the aspect of the Kingdom we are now considering. In the light of the Bible, there is a vast realm of evil, affecting everyone and to which everyone contributes. It is organised under a head, Satan, and it has its powerful, subtle strategy, and its periods of advance and retreat. But it is not to be so for ever and ever.

The Church needs to take more seriously than it has done in modern times all that the New Testament has to say about the evil powers. The whole armour of God is required that we "may be able to stand against the wiles of the devil; for we wrestle not against flesh and blood, but against principalities, against powers, against the rulers of the darkness of this world, against spiritual wickedness in high places" (Ephesians 6, 11–12). Over against all this, Christ thought of a Kingdom the full blessings of which lay beyond this scene in a transcendent and everlasting order. All the forces of evil will then be defeated and destroyed, and all who have bowed in penitent, willing, loving surrender before the Father-King revealed in the Son will inherit eternal life. Some true foretaste of the blessedness of that order can be known now, but we have to await the complete experience till we have entered through the gates of death.

It is in relation to this aspect of the Kingdom that we must interpret "the parables of crisis"—the faithful and unfaithful servants (Matthew 24, 45–51), the waiting servants (Luke 12, 35–38; Mark 13, 32–37), the thief at midnight (Matthew 24, 42–44), and the ten virgins (Matthew 25, 1–13). Paul is completely loyal to Jesus' teaching here, for he has the same emphasis (1 Thessalonians 5, 2–8; Ephesians 5, 8–14; 2 Corinthians 6, 2; 11, 2). It is difficult to believe that Jesus Himself regarded the "end" as imminent, in the sense that the early Church may have done; for in that case He would be mistaken, as the "end" has not yet come. The immediate interpretation of these parables and other sayings may have dominated the mind of His disciples for a time, but that does not imply that that was the total meaning of these parables and sayings for Jesus Himself. Indeed the larger, longer meanings put into them by the Church, as time passed, represent the drawing out in a fuller sense of what He intended when He spoke them. The developed doctrine of the Church, both in its evolutionary and eschatological sense, is implicit in His words—a just deduction, not a misleading departure. To study the parables of our Lord in their historical background, their "setting in life", is a most valuable and indispensable exercise; but we have to guard against its becoming an obsession and a bondage. Nevertheless, Jesus looked forward to the triumph of a Heavenly Feast, and in that context we have to set the parable of the Great Feast (Matthew 22, 1–14). Jesus told His disciples at the table in the upper room that he would "drink no more of the fruit of the vine until that day that I drink it new in the Kingdom of God" (Mark 14, 25). This most likely refers to the great Heavenly Feast, the new wine of the Kingdom. But the possibility of a more immediate reference cannot be excluded—a post-Resurrection fellowship with His disciples; for Peter, in his discourse with Cornelius, does not hesitate to say that the Risen Christ did eat and drink with them (Acts 10, 41). This final triumph is the Kingdom that "cannot be shaken" (Hebrews 12, 2).

The process of overcoming the Kingdom of Satan may be slow, but there will be a final separation of the wheat and the tares (Matthew 13, 24–30, 37–43). This problem of the slowness of the victory of good was a leading preoccupation of the writers of the apocalypses which appeared in the period between the Testaments. Paul interprets the ultimate end of the process as victory achieved by Christ over all His enemies, death included, as the prelude to "God being all in all" (1 Corinthians 15, 24–28). There is a special place of honour in the future consummation for the disciples (Matthew 19, 28).

5

In turning now to the third aspect of New Testament teaching on the Kingdom, we have to regard the recovery of the eschatological character of the Kingdom as a most welcome development, and a much-needed corrective to those tendencies in theology which exalted natural law, scientific causality and evolutionary process to such an elevation that the Kingdom seemed to be the achievement of man's effort, to be secured simply by the spread of ethical principles and their this-worldly applications. In the tumult and disorder which are never far from this world's life, amid which we are never permitted to think in terms of perfection here, faith is nourished by the assurance of God's final, glorious victory.

Theology, however, like all forms of human thought, is exposed to the danger of presenting itself in too sharp, and therefore false, antitheses. In large tracts of the Church's life in the past, and to a lesser degree in the present, there is much that is bleak and forbidding, because powerful tensions have been allowed to develop where there was no need for them. Aggressive controversy has frequently taken place between people who used the same terms but attach very different meanings to them. There is always a strong tendency among certain Christians to exhibit the martyr spirit where no martyrdom is required. Others follow the device of setting up positions for fierce attack which very few of the opposite persuasion hold in the shape in which they are set up, while still others disastrously fail to distinguish between principles, preferences and prejudices and consequently invest the preferences and prejudices with the once-for-all, untouchable sanctity which properly belongs to principles. It would be a notable gain for the Church in its evangelism if its different denominations and parties were to show themselves as enthusiastic and excited about all that they hold in common as they do about all that so sharply divides them. There is a sensitive and sensible equilibrium required in these matters. Lest it be thought that this is the peculiar sin of the Church, it should be added that it is often the same in other fields of study too. There is just as much extreme one-sidedness on the part of the modern humanist (who, on important issues of theology or philosophy, is often half a century behind the times) as on the part of the most hidebound, sectarian theologian.

Of course, there are true, irreconcilable antitheses. The very quintessence of the Bible is in the form "either—or." Ultimately there is only one scriptural antithesis—believe unto eternal life or perish. Throughout the Bible there is a clear call to choice—"life and good, or death and evil." (Deuteronomy 30, 15–20). We hear it resounding from Abraham, through Moses, Joshua, Elijah, and all the prophets, until John the Baptist. The decisive choice is evoked by God's prior action, and its character is always a response to what God has already done for us. His offers are marvellous but He never subjects Himself to the commands of men. The call for decision reaches its most urgent and personal form in the Gospel of Christ—"he that believeth on the Son hath everlasting life; and he that believeth not the Son shall not see life, but the wrath of God abideth on him." (John 3, 36). In this connection there are two sayings of Jesus which appear to cancel each other out—

"He that is not for me is against me." (Matthew 12, 30).

"He that is not against us is for us." (Luke 9, 50). But the contradiction disappears if we regard the former as the word to be used when we are judging ourselves, and the latter as the word to be used when we are judging others. For ourselves we need the more stringent, exacting word, for others the easier, gentler word. We should always seek for excuses for others and give them the benefit of every doubt, while it is always perilous to do that for ourselves. This is surely a point in life where the natural man takes just the opposite road. There are large areas of life where neutrality is only a deceptive appearance, where we have to take sides, and where failure to be on the right side is tantamount to being on the wrong side. The Gospel simply cannot be preached at all without presenting the antitheses of light and darkness, liberty and bondage, the new man and the old man, grace and law, Christ and all possible substitutes, the Kingdom of God and the kingdom of evil. Tolerance is a virtue, but it can be overdone.

At the same time, there often emerges a false dualism which, in the interests of truth and evangelism, we have to strive to transcend. In the many-sided discussion regarding Church reunion the false antithesis is continually raising its ugly head. They are optimists indeed who imagine that solutions in this field will be of an "either—or" character, and not "both—and," as if true catholicity were to be identified with any existing Church structure. The same kind of unwarranted antithesis marks a great deal of current discussion on the inspiration and authority of the Bible. In the field of theology too, when all allowance is made for the essential paradox of the Gospel, the eternal "either—or" which lies at the basis of all Christian belief, harm has been done by too sharp, mutually exclusive statements. Some examples of this are the relationship of prophet and priest, the manhood and the divinity of Jesus Christ, the place of belief and action in the Christian life, the sacramental principle and personal commitment, and the bearing of the eschatological hope on the so-called social Gospel. In all these and similar cases, it has to be stressed that the link between theology and evangelism is integral. Theology does not have an existence in its own full right, for there can be no irreverence so great as the dispassionate, disinterested and undirected discussion of God by man. Doctrine is there to be preached and a doctrine that cannot be preached is not likely to be sound. A theologian who is not much interested in preaching is a poor theologian. There is, of course, an overflow of clarification and enrichment from preaching into theology. The Church in every age has to go to its vital task with a theology which is capable of being the instrument of conversion.

It is in the field of eschatology, however, that the false antithesis most prominently appears. Realized eschatology and futurist eschatology have both shown a strong tendency to one-sided exclusiveness, and so our understanding of the mind of our Lord is distorted. During the war Professor Oscar Cullmann wrote a masterly and rousing book entitled "Christ and Time." One of the main strands in his basic argument is that in the long campaign of good against evil there are two focal points—D Day, when vast and decisive action takes place, and V Day, the day of final triumph. D Day is never V Day, but all that happens then guarantees the perhaps far-off victory. For the Christian pattern D Day is the Incarnation of our Lord, His death, resurrection and ascension; V Day is the Second Coming of Christ. Human history is not to go meandering and meandering for ever and ever. It had a definite beginning, hidden in the mists of remote antiquity; and it will have a definite "end," and Christ will be there in power and glory. But the interim is very long and the Christian religion does not stand aloof from it. We have to prepare the way of the Lord by bringing His practical teaching on the Kingdom into every generation and age until the "end" comes.

There are certain parables which make quite clear the double aspect of the Kingdom. There are the parables which are usually known as the parables of growth, such parables as those of The Seed Growing Secretly (Mark 4, 26–29); The Leaven (Matthew 13, 33); The Wheat and the Tares (Matthew 13, 24–30); The Mustard Seed (Matthew 13, 31, 32). All these parables say three things:

(1) Just because they are parables of growth, and just because they speak of the Kingdom in terms of the growth of nature, they do represent the coming of the Kingdom as a process and a development. Night and day, even when the farmer is asleep, the seed is growing secretly with an innate power within itself (Mark 4, 27). In the dough the leaven is

working, even if we can no more see it working than we can see a bulb growing (Matthew 13, 33). The growth of the Kingdom stands for the long working out of the design and purpose of God.

(2) Equally these parables say that something *has* happened. The farmer puts in the sickle because the harvest *has come* (Mark 4, 29). As C. H. Dodd has pointed out, there is a sense in which the action of leaven is anything but unseen, for the leaven turns the dough into a bubbling, seething, heaving mass There is a real sense in which the work of the leaven is typified in the action on society of those who have turned the world upside down. (Acts 17, 6). With the coming of Jesus something happened; the Kingdom in a unique sense *came*.

(3) These parables declare that something *will* happen. They look to a harvest which will also be a judgment, when the wheat and the tares will be separated, and when each will go to their own place (Matthew 13:30); they look to a time when all nations will be gathered in, for in Eastern thought the symbol of a great empire is the picture of many birds finding their shelter in the branches of some great tree (Matthew 13, 32).

In the parables of growth we see the Kingdom as something which continues to happen, something which has happened, and something which will in the end come to a final consummation.

It is scarcely true to say that the Kingdom of God is confined to heaven. It is fully there; here it is imperfectly disclosed. We have to work and pray to remove the difference between heaven and earth, to make earth "a colony of heaven," with all that that implies. But indeed there have been some brave, consistent and successful attempts to obey the will of God on the part of individuals and sometimes even by society. In these we have a forecast and a foretaste of what earth might become if God's law became universal. In Jesus we have a living picture of what life in heaven would be like; and if we want to know that better we should study Him more. Our task is to bring heaven to earth—stupendous indeed but not impossible. Jesus says it can be done, else He would never have put it in His model prayer. "Thy will be done on earth as it is in heaven." Too often in the mood of feeble acquiescence do we say "Thy will be done." Too often we imply, "Let it be done in spite of us, even against our wills, and we will try to bear it." But this is not what the prayer means. "Let it be done by us; let us brace ourselves chivalrously and eagerly to follow it—not merely enduring the will of God as sufferers but doing it as active service." It is not a motto for a cemetery but a badge of action.

In certain circumstances Christian resignation is a fine and noble thing—the calm and meek way in which some people bear themselves in situations where there is nothing to be done, such as loss of fortune, health or friends. It may be that the only way then is to be submissive and resigned. The Christian type of resignation, as against other types, is beautiful. But there is something in this prayer for the happy, alert and strong as well as for the mourner, the invalid and the infirm; something for all times, not merely for times of trouble. This was how Jesus lived His own life—realising the Father's will at every stage and in all circumstances. It is a false resignation which acquiesces in evil things which God wants removed. For then indeed not resignation but rebellion is needed if God's will is to be done. Robert Louis Stevenson says to his old gardener: "There is a plant called wintergreen or Resignation, a strong plant but of no profit. I will not have it in my garden: root it out!"

But, of course, Christianity is not merely for the individual. Christ has a programme for the world, something He offers through us—a new world order. At different times He emphasised different aspects of the coming of the Kingdom: but clearly it involves this too. Some there are who would suggest that a new world order was never part of His intention, so that we cannot hope for the establishment of righteousness and peace. "When comes the promised time. . . . ?" "Never," they say, "because it was never promised." All He hopes to do is to gather the saved out of a perishing world. The world may perish, may go from bad to worse till final ruin is reached. But that this is not what God intended is shown by Christ's first sermon at Nazareth (Luke 4, 16–20). Here the key words are: "He hath anointed me" and "He hath sent me." Christ is always conscious of a mission. He has been sent for a purpose. God knows all about this world and everything in it which makes the life of men and women more difficult—its wrongs, oppressions, sufferings and injustices. That in itself ought to bring hope to those who are the victims of these things. Never should the blasphemy be uttered that these things are the will of God. On the contrary, men ought always to be in rebellion against them, working hard for their removal, never content to leave things as they are.

So, in this "Announcement at Nazareth" we have the proclamation of a new world for the poor—there will be no under-privileged class in the Kingdom—and good news for the suffering and the oppressed.

The Christian has a practical duty, not so much to understand suffering as to alleviate it, not so much to explain it as to lessen it, not so much to diagnose it as to defeat it. Probably we cannot say that a world free from suffering is conceivable. Paul apparently did not think it possible. The promise of no more pain does not refer to this world and this earthly state. Yet, if we believe Jesus, the burden can be greatly lessened.

For this, supremely, our Lord gave Himself. He was bruised to heal our bruises, wounded to cure our wounds. "To Jesus," says Professor J. S. Stewart, "God's will was everything. It was God's will that the world should be redeemed; and if the achievement of that redemption lay on the road of the supreme sacrifice, then welcome death! That was Jesus' spirit. He loved life dearly but He loved God's will far more." *

* *The Life and Teaching of Jesus Christ.*

Christ is distinguished from all who have merely given programmes for the world. He gave Himself for it. He died for it, confident that death would not break or defeat but crown His purpose. In this joy which was set before Him He endured the Cross. And to those who follow after Him comes the great discovery that no cross need defeat them, no burden need crush them, no suffering need rob them of faith in a Father. Christ died and lives to bear every cross, lift every load, and to give in all conditions the spirit of serene content.

But how is Christ's programme to be carried into effect? That is always an urgent question. Many may say they quite agree that the teaching is right and all that it implies is sound and desirable but that humanly speaking it is impossible. If we face it with merely human resources, we shall be able to go only a small distance; we shall only potter at the immense job of building the new order.

Our great need is the Spirit of God. We need faith: "The Spirit of the Lord is upon me; He hath sent me to preach the acceptable year of the Lord." A reformer who is not a deeply religious man may do much for the good of the world in his own way. But God's choice instrument for the Kingdom is the life in which His Spirit dwells and works. And Jesus said the Father would give the Spirit to all who asked for Him.

What, then, do we mean by the Spirit of God? How do we receive Him? The foundation of all belief and all service is the assurance that there is a God who knows and watches and has a plan for the world. Without this nothing we attempt to build will stand: without this life is robbed of its meaning. The more we think of it the more intolerable becomes the idea that this life of ours and the world of which it is a part have no meaning—are just accidents, governed by the most random chance and leading nowhere. But the truest and most satisfying interpretation of life declares that there is a personal God with a Mind which knows and purposes, a Heart which loves and a Will which works. When we say that we need the Spirit of God, we mean that we need to live in such close touch with God that He influences, guides, inspires, and fills us with enthusiasm. It is by no random wish that we can live thus. It means earnest dedication. It means a disciplined devotional life.

What will give the world a new start? Christ's message in this passage suggests the answer. We need a revival of religion, faith, hope, love reborn. History verifies the truth of this: witness the Reformation or the Wesleyan revival. Every time the world has taken a big step forward has been a time of large returning to God; and it may confidently be prophesied that the next big step forward will be of the same character, when a new spirit, even the Spirit of God, grips the people.

The Spirit of God, bringing energy and courage, is not given to people who really do not want such a gift. God knows perfectly well how much or how little we want it and whether we are prepared to do the obeying and the sacrifice which are always involved. The Spirit came in amazing fulness upon the first apostles, precisely because they were utterly surrendered men. The world is full of social wrongs which we cannot put right of ourselves. Some indeed would maintain that we ought to put the social wrongs right first and then when we have thus put our house in order God will give us the Spirit and carry us forward. This is a quite mistaken view. We need desperately the help of God's Spirit to put right our social wrongs. Without God in our life none of us can care for others in Christ's deep, compassionate way. It is the Spirit of God who makes us care; it is the Spirit of God who gives our conscience no rest; it is the Spirit of God who keeps reminding us that there is "something rotten in the state of Denmark." If we are to put the world right, we must come to love even the sinful, misguided people who are putting it wrong; but the simple fact is that we cannot love other people and go on loving them when we find them out, unless we love God first. Without the faith of Christ we cannot begin to tackle this stupendous task at all. It is quite certain that there is no way out of the world's misery except the way Jesus showed—love, unselfishness, patience, service; and these are the fruits of the Spirit of God.

Some may bypass religion and still hope to achieve the same results which faith in Christ offers, to gather the fruits of the Spirit without the Spirit. They look around the world and see so much that needs to be put right—poor to be relieved, oppressed and downtrodden to be set free, injustices and inequalities to be removed. They work for a time and then all too often grow tired or even cynical—it seems a hopeless task—and like Bertrand Russell they reconcile themselves to that "unyielding despair" on which nothing positive can be built. They are trying to make the new world out of human resources only; they want the Kingdom of God without God; and it simply cannot be done. The power and dynamic of the Spirit are wanting.

Others again may think to find God in a self-centred mysticism that ignores the world and its crying ills. They wallow in the comfort of religion devoid of practical results. Both extremes are wrong. The truth is that you cannot be of real, creative use to other people unless you have God in your life; and when you have God in your life you cannot help caring for serving other people.

In the last resort there is a strong possibility of a Kingdom of God on earth because the Resurrection of our Lord is a fact. It declares a great mystery. (Romans 16, 25–27). By the Resurrection the whole Old Testament preparation is unfolded and understood. By it God exposes and reverses the desires of blind, unteachable, envious and evil men when they brought Jesus to Calvary. By it also we are enabled to see how this cruel Cross is something undertaken by the Son for the sin of all men. By it we have our one and only assurance of resurrection from the dead. But there is more than all that. It was the power of God which raised His Son and gave Him glory. Here on a miraculous scale the power of God breaks through into history and does mighty acts. One of the great Christian certainties, which is not taken with sufficient seriousness, is that God Himself is available in the power of the Resurrection. According to our faith, obedience and sacrifice we can have that power when we are engaged on the work of the Kingdom. Obviously this Kingdom needs new men and women. Accordingly, the Christian Church, deeply anchored in the New Testament, must never weary of calling for conversion as something that all men and women require, without which the deepest joys of life cannot be tasted nor its highest victories won.

"And this gospel of the kingdom shall be preached in all the world for a witness unto all nations; and then shall the end come."

(Matthew 24, 14)

"Then cometh the end, when he shall have delivered up the kingdom to God, even the Father; when he shall have put down all rule and all authority and power. For he must reign, till he hath put all enemies under his feet. The last enemy that shall be destroyed is death. For he hath put all things under his feet. But when he saith all things are put under him, it is manifest that he is excepted, which did put all things under him. And when all things shall be subdued unto him, then shall the Son also himself be subject unto him that put all things under him, that God may be all in all."

(1 Corinthians 15, 24–28)